EAST ASIAN SOCIETIES

Key Issues in Asian Studies, No. 14

AAS Resources for Teaching About Asia

EAST ASIAN SOCIETIES

W. LAWRENCE NEUMAN

Association for Asian Studies, Inc.
825 Victors Way, Suite 310
Ann Arbor, MI 48108 USA
www.asian-studies.org

KEY ISSUES IN ASIAN STUDIES

A series edited by Lucien Ellington, University of Tennessee at Chattanooga

"Key Issues" volumes complement the Association for Asian Studies' teaching journal, *Education About Asia*—a practical teaching resource for secondary school, college, and university instructors, as well as an invaluable source of information for students, scholars, libraries, and those who have an interest in Asia.

Formed in 1941, the Association for Asian Studies (AAS)—the largest society of its kind, with approximately 8,000 members worldwide—is a scholarly, non-political, non-profit professional association open to all persons interested in Asia.

For further information, please visit www.asian-studies.org

Copyright © 2014 by the Association for Asian Studies, Inc.

Published by the Association for Asian Studies, Inc. All Rights Reserved. Written permission must be secured to use or reproduce any part of this book.

For orders or inquiries, please contact:
Association for Asian Studies, Inc.
825 Victors Way, Suite 310
Ann Arbor, MI 48108 USA
Tel: (734) 665-2490
Fax: (734) 665-3801
www.asian-studies.org

Library of Congress Cataloging-in-Publication Data

Neuman, William Lawrence, 1950–
East Asian societies / W. Lawrence Neuman.
    pages cm. — (Key issues in Asian studies ; No. 14)
Includes bibliographical references.
    ISBN 978-0-924304-74-3 (pbk. : alk. paper) 1. East Asia—History. 2. East Asia—Civilization. 3. East Asia—Social conditions. 4. East Asia—Economic conditions. I. Title.
    DS511.N43 2014
    950—dc23
                            2014004178

To my father

About "Key Issues in Asian Studies"

Key Issues in Asian Studies (*KIAS*) volumes engage major cultural and historical themes in the Asian experience. *Key Issues* books complement the Association for Asian Studies' teaching journal, *Education About Asia*, and serve as vital educational materials that are both accessible and affordable for classroom use.

Key Issues books tackle broad subjects or major events in an introductory but compelling style appropriate for survey courses. Although authors of the series have distinguished themselves as scholars as well as teachers, the prose style employed is accessible for broad audiences. This series is particularly intended for teachers and undergraduates at two- and four-year colleges as well as advanced high school students and secondary school teachers engaged in teaching Asian studies in a comparative framework and anyone with an interest in Asia.

For further information about *Key Issues in Asian Studies*, *Education About Asia*, or the Association for Asian Studies, visit www.asian-studies.org.

Prospective authors interested in *Key Issues in Asian Studies* or *Education About Asia* are encouraged to contact:

> Lucien Ellington, University of Tennessee at Chattanooga
> Tel: (423) 425-2118; E-Mail: Lucien-Ellington@utc.edu

"Key Issues" volumes available from AAS:

> *Confucius in East Asia* by Jeffrey L. Richey
>
> *The Story of Việt Nam: From Prehistory to the Present* by Shelton Woods
>
> *Modern Chinese History* by David Kenley
>
> *Korea in World History* by Donald N. Clark
>
> *Traditional China in Asian and World History* by Tansen Sen and Victor Mair
>
> *Zen Past and Present* by Eric Cunningham
>
> *Japan and Imperialism*, 1853–1945 by James L. Huffman
>
> *Japanese Popular Culture and Globalization* by William M. Tsutsui
>
> *Global India circa 100 CE: South Asia in Early World History* by Richard H. Davis
>
> *Caste in India* by Diane Mines
>
> *Understanding East Asia's Economic "Miracles"* by Zhiqun Zhu
>
> *Political Rights in Post-Mao China* by Merle Goldman
>
> *Gender, Sexuality, and Body Politics in Modern Asia* by Michael Peletz

ABOUT THE AUTHOR

W. LAWRENCE NEUMAN is Professor of Sociology at the University of Wisconsin, Whitewater where he chairs the Department of Sociology, Anthropology, and Criminal Justice and is coordinator of the Japanese Studies and Asian Studies programs. He has a PhD from the University of Wisconsin. His teaching and research interests are in East Asia, especially issues of inequality, civil society, and identity in Japan. His writings on Asia have appeared in the *Journal of Contemporary Asia, Social Science Japan, Critical Asian Studies*, and *Japan Studies Journal*. His recent books include *Basics of Social Research*, 3rd ed.; *Social Research Methods*, 7th ed.; *Understanding Research*; and *Power, State, and Society*. His sociology research articles have appeared in *Social Problems, Sociological Inquiry, Sociological Quarterly, Social Science Quarterly, Sociological Imagination, Law and Society Review, Teaching Sociology*, and *American Sociological Review*.

CONTENTS

Acknowledgments / xi

Editor's Introduction / xiii

Introduction / 1

1. **East Asian History / 5**
China before European Conquest / 5
Japan before Western Contact / 12
Korea before Japanese Control / 17
The Rise of Imperial Japan / 19
After the Pacific War / 21
Conclusion / 23

2. **East Asian Culture / 25**
The Ways of Culture / 25
Three Traits of Culture / 28
Is There an East Asian Culture? / 29
China (Sino) Civilization and Confucius / 30
Daoism / 33
Buddhism / 34
Ghosts, Oracles, Shamanism, and Shintō / 36
Other Cultural Practices / 37
Dynamic Youth Culture / 38
Conclusion / 38

3. **Family Life in East Asia / 39**
The Ideal Family / 39
Real Families / 41
Filial Piety and Ancestors / 42
Courtship, Spouse Selection, and Marriage / 43

Family Registration / 45

Child Rearing and Multigenerational Households / 47

Housework / 49

Conclusion / 51

4.   **School and the Transition to Work / 53**
Schooling Differences / 53

The Examination System / 58

Country Differences / 62

School-to-Work Linkages / 64

Conclusion / 66

5.   **Inequality and Diversity in East Asia / 67**
Racial-Ethnic Diversity / 67

Gender Inequality / 73

China's "Missing Girls" / 74

Social Class and Economic Inequality / 75

Urban-Rural Inequality / 81

Conclusion / 85

6.   **Looking to the Future / 87**
Economic Growth / 87

Global Connections / 92

Social Adjustments / 95

Nationalism and National Identity / 97

Conclusion / 102

Notes / 103

Glossary / 117

Suggestions for Further Reading / 123

Acknowledgments

This booklet is the culmination of fifteen years of teaching and writing on East Asia. I am especially grateful to the Fulbright program and for support received from the Freeman Foundation, National Science Foundation, National Endowment for the Humanities, U.S. Department of Education, the Japanese government's MEXT (Ministry of Education, Culture, Sports, Science & Technology) and the Asian Studies Development Program at the East-West Center.

I would also like to thank Tohoku University, Kansai Gakuin University, Nankai University, the University of Hawaii, and the University of Wisconsin–Whitewater for their support. I benefited from stimulating discussions at the Japan Studies Association, Midwest Japan Seminar, AsianNetwork, and the Midwest Conference on Asia Affairs. Many people have taught me about East Asia, including Betty Buck, Roger Ames, Thomas Kasulis, Peter Hershock, Ruth Grubel, Wade Dazey, Jian Guo, Kasumi Kato, Masako Lackey, Xia Li Lollar, Herman Smith, Hajimu Sasaki, Laura Miller, Louis Perez, Wayne Patterson, Jeffrey Broadbent, Joseph Overton, Richard Coughlin, Mary Brinton, Yoshimichi Sato, Yoichi Murase, and Apichai Shipper.

I also want to thank the two reviewers of my original manuscript. They gave it a careful reading and offered many excellent suggestions. Special thanks must go to Lucien Ellington, who has not only been an outstanding editor but remains a passionate champion for Asian studies, whose mixture of humor, wit, and professionalism is unmatched.

Editor's Introduction

Lawrence Neuman's *East Asian Societies* is a welcome addition to the *Key Issues in Asian Studies* (*KIAS*) series for several reasons. *East Asian Societies* is the first volume in the series authored by a sociologist and is an ideal addition for introductory university and high school surveys of that discipline. However, the different cultures and topics included in *East Asian Societies*, as well as the book's readability and overall quality mean that undergraduate and high school students in a broad array of disciplines and subjects ranging from human geography to introduction to Asia courses will gain a solid basic understanding of East Asia if they are fortunate enough to read this work.

Writing a useful and interesting but succinct treatment of five different societies is no easy task, but long term professional interactions with and admiration of Larry Neuman made me confident from the beginning of our conversations about a *Key Issues* society volume that he could make an excellent contribution to the series. Professor Neuman and I first met in 1997 when we participated in an East-West Center Korean studies program and study tour. Larry's intellectual curiosity, love of East Asia, upbeat "can do" attitude, and work ethic were quickly apparent to me. In the ensuing years as Larry made several outstanding contributions to the *Education About Asia* journal, I was also impressed by the lucidity and accessibility of his prose. Larry has a reputation as an outstanding scholar of sociology and of Japan, as a leader in Asian studies education at the undergraduate level, and perhaps is even better known in his field as the author of two introductory works in his discipline. Their success with instructors and students is apparent based upon the multiple editions of each book published.

To put it another way, based on my experiences working with Larry on the volume I am convinced the typical 19 year old, or anyone unfamiliar with East Asian society, will not be able to find a more useful introduction to the topic than the work you hold in your hands.

As is always the case, the successful development of this volume would have been impossible without the help of several people. Montgomery

Broaded read the initial proposal, and he and Carol Stepanchuk served as external referees for the manuscript. Both the author and I appreciated their thoughtful suggestions. Special thanks also go to Charlotte Hill, who is a University of Tennessee at Chattanooga honors student with a deep interest in East Asia. Charlotte was an intern in our office when this manuscript was developed and provided invaluable comments on various chapters.

Finally, I am deeply grateful to Jonathan Wilson, AAS Publications Manager and to the AAS Editorial Board for their strong support of pedagogical initiatives such as *Education About Asia* and *Key Issues in Asian Studies*.

Lucien Ellington
Series Editor, Key Issues in Asian Studies

INTRODUCTION

Most Americans view the "Orient," "Far East," or East Asia through a lens of films, news reports, Asian restaurants, or products from Asia. To many the collage of images, smells, tastes, and sounds appears exotic or mysterious. For over a century, Americans and other westerners spoke of East Asia as being strange, baffling, or inscrutable. For almost as long, politicians evoked fear and anxiety regarding East Asia, using scare phrases such as "Yellow Peril" to describe people coming from Asia. Today anxieties about Asian economic power or political influence persist.

Many other Americans are intrigued and curious about Asian languages, music, martial arts, medical practices such as acupuncture, religious beliefs, and foods. Today many drive a Japanese- or Korean-made car, watch a Korean-made television, use a laptop with an LCD screen from Taiwan, watch anime or play video games created in Japan, or taste versions of Chinese dishes in local food courts. On a daily basis what we use—refrigerators to gym shorts to sushi—comes from East Asia. Yet few of us truly understand the peoples and societies of this major world region.

Outsiders—the ancient Greeks—created the very idea of Asia and drew arbitrary lines on a map to define it. Asia was not a coherent place or self-identity for most Asian people until the beginning of the last century. "Many politicians, bureaucrats, journalists, business peoples (and academics) write and talk about Asia as if there was a physical or cultural reality that corresponds to that term" (Birch, Schirato, and Srivastava 2001, 1). Stereotypes used to classify Asian people began in an era of European and American explorers, colonialists, and traders, and by later military or business strategists. They sought to simplify and organize impressions of a distant, foreign region.

Asia is a huge geographic world region subdivided into West (Middle East), Central, South, Southeast, and East Asia. We focus on East Asia (or geographically the Northeast) in this book. East Asia has five countries: the People's Republic of China (PRC), the Republic of China (Taiwan), Japan, the Republic of Korea (South Korea), and the Democratic People's Republic of Korea (North Korea). Note that the PRC does not consider Taiwan to be a separate nation but considers it legally part of China. Also, since it is very difficult to obtain reliable information on North Korea, this book has little on that reclusive society.

Peoples of the region have interacted with each other for centuries. Despite the proximity, they have distinct traditions, customs, languages, and political systems. They differ from one another as much as Mexico, Jamaica, United States, and Brazil differ but are linked by history and culture. In this book you will learn what East Asian societies share in common and how they differ from one another.

A good starting place is to look at the map opposite. You quickly see that two countries are islands (or an island chain), two are on a peninsula, and the other covers much of a continent. The countries are unequal in geographic size. China has the fourth-largest land area of all nations in the world and is slightly smaller than the United States in terms of total area (which includes bodies of water). Taiwan is the smallest. It is about the size of the state of Maryland. South Korea is almost three times larger than Taiwan, about the size of Indiana. North and South Korea combined are the size of Wyoming. The islands of Japan are close in size to California.

The countries border the Pacific Ocean or its seas (e.g., the East China Sea). Except in the interior regions of vast China, most East Asians are not far from the sea. The climate varies greatly. To the northwest is Siberia. It brings bitter cold winters with snow in the northern regions. The far southern regions of China are tropical, but most of East Asia has four seasons. Summers tend to be hot and humid with a rainy season in June, often including typhoons, but winters are dry.

East Asia is mountainous, and many of the mountains are volcanoes. This part of the world is geologically unstable with frequent earthquakes. The many mountains, closeness to a sea, and frequent earthquakes have shaped beliefs and traditions in the region.

About one in four people on the earth live in East Asia, but populations vary by country. You probably know that China is the world's most populous nation, but Japan is currently ranked as the tenth largest. South

2

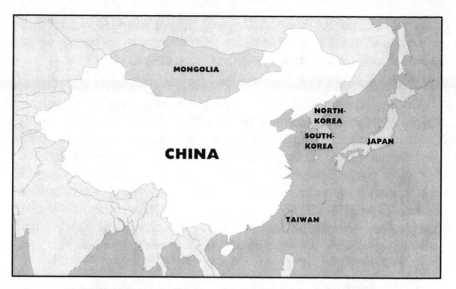

Map I.1. East Asia. Source: http://www.freeworldmaps.net
/asia/eastasia/pdf.html. Accessed January 26, 2014.

Korea has about as many people as Spain, and North Korea and Taiwan each have populations roughly equal that of Australia. Three countries (Japan, South Korea, and Taiwan) have high population densities.

Population growth was fast across East Asia before the 1970s. It has since slowed, and population size has stabilized. Today Japan has negative population growth, and growth is nearly zero in South Korea and Taiwan. As growth slowed, the age mix of people changed. Because Japan, Taiwan, South Korea, and China grew rapidly in the 1950s–60s, they had many

Table I.1. Summary of East Asian Geography and Democracy

Country	Land Area (sq km)	Population	Population Growth Rate (%)	Population Density (per sq. km)
China	9,569,901	1.33 billion	0.49	138
Taiwan	32,260	23.02 million	0.21	713
South Korea	96,920	48.64 million	0.26	502
North Korea	120,408	22.76 million	0.39	189
Japan	364,485	126.80 million	-0.24	348
USA (for Comparison)	9,161,966	310.23 million	0.97	34

young adults in the 1980s–90s. This group of people tended to marry late and have small families. All East Asian populations are now moving in the same direction—an increasingly high percentage of elderly people. As you will see in the last chapter, this is a major social issue in East Asia.

Six decades ago most East Asian people lived in small towns or rural villages. The trend, especially in the past three to five decades, has been to move into cities. Today East Asian societies are urbanized and home to four of the world's ten largest cities. The Tokyo metropolitan area has about thirty-two million people, making it the world's largest city. Seoul, South Korea, is the world's second-largest city with over twenty million residents. Eleven Chinese cities have over six million people (the United States has just one city that large; New York). Taipei, on the small island nation of Taiwan, has twelve million, which is nearly one-half of all the people in the country.

Because the East Asian region encompasses a heritage going back to antiquity, to understand contemporary East Asia it is important for us to become acquainted with its historical context. This constitutes the focus of chapter 1. After a review of the region's history, we turn to its cultural traditions and belief systems in chapter 2. Next, in chapter 3, we consider a core institution that has an especially significant place in East Asian societies—the family. In chapter 4 we move outside the family sphere to look at two areas of life that shape the individual and reveal societal forces—school and work. Social diversity and inequality in East Asian societies are the focus of chapter 5. In the final chapter, we look toward the future of the East Asian region by considering four overlapping themes: economic growth, globalization, societal adjustment, and nationalism.

1

EAST ASIAN HISTORY

For most Americans, East Asian history begins with the Second World War when Japan attacked Pearl Harbor in 1941 or with the Korean War in 1950 when communists from the north invaded the south. This is understandable but incomplete. East Asia's history is far longer and richer. More significantly, it continues to influence life in East Asia today.

CHINA BEFORE EUROPEAN CONQUEST

Homo sapiens came out of Africa about one hundred thousand years ago. Humans migrated to the Middle East about ninety thousand years ago, and early civilizations appeared in the eastern Mediterranean. Migrations continued eastward. People arrived in East Asia about sixty thousand years ago and built new civilizations. East Asian civilizations thrived centuries before the Christian era in the West.[1]

We begin with China, which has the oldest records. Early Chinese history was a sequence of dynasties (a leader with ruling families; see table 1.1), and written history starts with the Shang dynasty (seventeenth through eleventh centuries BCE). Scholars trace early forms of Chinese writing to this era. Significant Chinese culture, literature, and philosophy emerged in the eight-hundred-year-long Zhou dynasty (1045–256 BCE), which ranks as China's longest-lasting dynasty. Confucianism and Daoism (discussed in the next chapter) also emerged in the Zhou era. This occurred before the rise of Greek city-states such as Athens and Sparta, which many see as the start of western civilization. Thus, China had a sophisticated civilization for centuries before the famous Greek philosopher Plato walked the earth (ca. 428–347 BCE).

After a 250-year era of division and turmoil that historians have labeled the Warring States period, the Qin dynasty reunited China in 221

Table 1.1. Simplified List of Major Chinese Dynasties

Dynasty	Approximate Years
Shang	1600–1029 BCE
Zhou	1045–256 BCE
Warring States	475–221 BCE
Qin	221-206 BCE
Han	206 BCE–220 CE
Three Kingdoms	220–65
Jin	265–420
Southern and Northern	420–589
Sui	589–618
Tang	618–907
Five Dynasties and Ten Kingdoms	907–60
Song	960–1279
Liao, Jin, and Xia	907–1271 (overlap due to partial territory control)
Yuan "Great Khan"	1271–1368
Ming	1368–1644
Qing	1644–1911

BCE. The Qin dynasty consolidated territory and built China's first true empire. The emperor of the Qin standardized written Chinese characters, expanded irrigation and road building, established a clear legal code, created a common system of measurement and currency, and ordered the building of the Great Wall. People digging near the ancient Qin capital of Xi'an in 1974 uncovered the First Emperor's tomb. Inside they found a vast army of terracotta figures in excellent condition. There were 8,000 soldiers, 130 chariots with 520 horses, and 150 cavalry horses. This attests to a highly complex, sophisticated society in China over a century and a half prior to Julius Caesar and the rise of the Roman Empire.

The Qin dynasty was very short (221–206 BCE), but the Han dynasty that followed lasted until 220 CE. Han dynasty rulers were the first to embrace Confucianism, a philosophy that shaped Chinese society for over fifteen hundred years and continues to influence it today. The Chinese

Figure 1.1. The Great Wall of China (Author photo).

Figure 1.2. Terracotta army buried during the Qin dynasty. Source:
http://commons.wikimedia.org/wiki/File:Terracottaarmyxx.jpg.

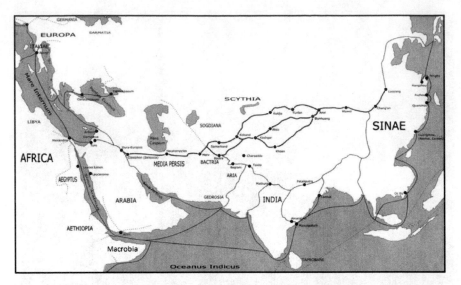

Map 1.1. Silk Roads, 1 CE. Source: http://commons.wikimedia.org/wiki/
File:Transasia_trade_routes_1stC_CE_gr2.png.

empire grew outward to what is now Inner Mongolia and expanded to the shores of the Caspian Sea, which today borders Russia and Iran. As Han military missions pushed westward, they returned with new objects. Slowly, western trade routes opened connecting China to the Middle East and indirectly to Europe.

The Silk Roads were major trade routes encompassing over 3,000 miles that connected Asia with the Mediterranean civilizations. In addition to silk, people traded gold, ivory, exotic animals, and plants. The Silk Roads facilitated cultural, commercial, and technological exchange among traders, missionaries, soldiers, and nomads. They connected China with India, Persia, and the Mediterranean region for almost three thousand years. Buddhism spread from India to China in part through the Silk Roads. Later, Islam reached west China along the Silk Roads as well.

Internal divisions intensified near the end of the Han era, and Buddhism expanded throughout China in the later Han era. After the Han dynasty's collapse, the subsequent forty-five-year Three Kingdoms period was marked by disunity and warfare, and an estimated one-half of China's population perished in the turmoil. Slow recovery began under the Jin dynasty (265–420 CE), but during the Southern and Northern dynasties (420–589 CE), another era of fragmentation and warfare followed. Finally, the Sui dynasty (581–618 CE) emerged to consolidate and expand its borders. China's empire extended south to Vietnam, but attempts to conquer Korea were unsuccessful. The dynasty's most notable achievement was building the world's longest canal (1,103 miles). The Great Canal extended from near Beijing to south of Shanghai.

Eventually, the Tang dynasty (618–907 CE) arose to return China to its former glory. From its capital in Xi'an, the world's most populous city at the time, Tang rulers brought 250 years of progress and stability. China's arts and sciences advanced, poetry flourished among the educated elites, and the empire's population grew. The Tang state controlled more land area than any previous dynasty had. Its relative peace and prosperity supported a rich civilization and growing population. Massive armies enabled the empire to expand, protect the Silk Roads, and build a navy that sailed as far as the coast of East Africa. As trade relations expanded, thousands of merchants from present day Iran, India, Cambodia, Malaysia, and Vietnam settled in China. Jews, Christians, and Muslims traveled to China, adding to a dynamic, cosmopolitan way of life in cities and towns. During the Tang dynasty, elements of China's advanced culture, including its writing system, spread to Korea, Japan, and Vietnam.

A period of fragmentation, the Five Dynasties and Ten Kingdoms (907–60 CE) followed. Eventually, the Song dynasty (960–1279) emerged. Historians consider it to be strikingly modern, particularly its cities. During the Song era, China's governing structure changed significantly when most bureaucrats began to be selected based on examinations, and a sophisticated commerce system emerged, particularly during the late, or Southern Song, era.

Next a series of weak dynasties ruled China. This era of division and confusion gave the Mongols, people from the north of China, an opportunity. Led by Genghis Khan (i.e., Great Khan), the Mongols invaded the Chinese heartland, pillaging and killing as they took control. Before the Mongol invasion, China's population was about 120 million. By the time of the 1300 census, only roughly half that number remained. After the death of Genghis Kahn in 1227, the Mongols stayed, adopted Chinese customs, and ruled as the Yuan dynasty (1271–1368), the first dynasty to rule China from Peking (now Beijing).

The Yuan dynasty's territory was larger than that of the Roman Empire and stretched from China westward to Eastern Europe (Ukraine, Belarus, Lithuania, and Poland) and Iraq and south into Vietnam. The Yuan empire only lasted about one hundred years and collapsed after a series of natural disasters and frequent local uprisings. Skilled at conquest and expansion, the Mongols were not able to govern such a vast territory.

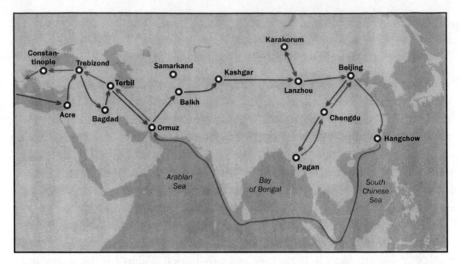

Map 1.2. Marco Polo's travels. Source: http://commons.wikimedia.org/wiki/
File:Travels_of_Marco_Polo.png.

A significant event in this period was travel by Marco Polo (1254–1324), a merchant from the city-state of Venice on the Italian peninsula. He traveled throughout Asia and lived in China for two decades, then returned to Europe with tales of China's riches.

The native Chinese Ming dynasty (1368–1644) replaced foreign warrior Mongols. It reoriented China toward agriculture, repaired the Great Wall, and encouraged trade again. The Ming expanded southward, conquering people of other ethnicities. As they incorporated new lands into their empire, large numbers of Chinese settlers followed. Under the Ming, the system of examinations for government service was revised, merchants increased in importance, and cities grew. The Ming capital was originally the city of Nanjing (known as the Southern Capital), but later it was moved 650 miles north to Beijing (Northern Capital). There the Ming reconstructed the city and placed a huge palace for the emperor, his assistants, and his family at the center—the Forbidden City. Today the Forbidden City—so named since all except the emperor's court, servants, and high-ranking imperial bureaucrats were forbidden to enter—is a leading tourist site in Beijing.

About 250 years after Marco Polo's travels, Europeans "discovered" East Asia, this time by sea. The Portuguese were the first Europeans to reach China, arriving in the southern port city of Guangzhou (old name Canton) in 1514. China's imperial court was not curious about the barbarian strangers who entered a remote region far from the capital and only requested tribute, as was the case for any foreigner. As happened in previous dynasties, the Ming eventually grew weak and faced growing internal strife. Once again outside invaders gained control. This time it was the Manchu, people from the separate kingdom of Manchuria, located northeast of China.

The Manchu, like the Mongols, were outsiders, not Han Chinese. Like the Mongols, the invading Manchu stayed, assimilated to Chinese culture, and ruled. The Qing (1644–1911) became China's last dynasty (a republican revolution in 1911 overthrew the regime). Relatively early in the Qing dynasty, the empire gained control over an island 112 miles from China's east coast that the Europeans had named Formosa or "Beautiful Island." The name of the island today is Taiwan. The Qing consolidated the south and west but during the nineteenth century their control over the vast territory of China weakened. During the two centuries between the Portuguese arrival and 1800, Europeans used their superior military technology to advance as they sought riches, trade, and religious converts from China.

Conflict erupted as Europeans continued to press for trade. They wanted silk, tea, porcelain, and other luxury goods that brought high profits at home. However, China wanted little that the Europeans had brought in exchange, so the Europeans turned to the addictive drug opium. The British shipped huge quantities of opium from their South Asian colonies. The Qing government objected and resisted opium imports. Tensions grew until Britain and China engaged in a series of Opium Wars. A first conflict (1839–42) was followed by another (1856–60) after a few years of peace. The British victors imposed fines, unequal treaties, and harsh conditions on the Qing, further weakening the government. By the mid-1800s, the country was a helpless giant overrun by westerners who had "carved up" China into many "spheres of influence." Large areas were under British, French, German, and Russian control. Later the Americans and Japanese joined in the scramble for wealth and resources in China. The outsiders imposed extraterritoriality, meaning foreigners were not subject to Chinese law or authorities. Instead, foreigners lived by their own laws while in China. Periodically, the humiliated Chinese people rebelled against the foreigners, but the 1850–64 Taiping Rebellion—the name means "Great Peace"—was a major civil war. The Taiping rebels opposed a weak, corrupt Qing dynasty that had allowed foreigners to overrun the country. The Qing government eventually defeated the rebels, but twenty million people died in the conflict. In 1898 the Boxer antiforeign movement arose. The Boxer Rebellion, too, was crushed by military force, this time by

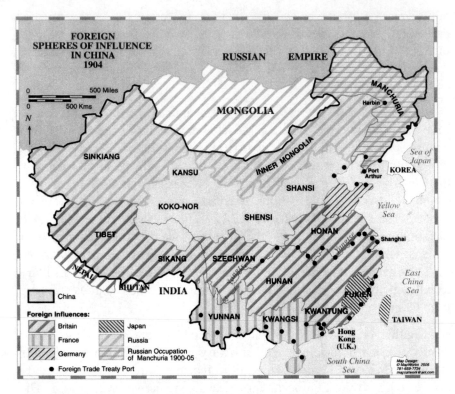

Map 1.3. Foreign spheres of influence in China, 1904. Map commissioned by
Japan-America Society of New Hampshire for Portsmouth Peace Treaty
website at portsmouthpeacetreaty.com. Map Design © MapWorks 2005,
MAPSatWORK@aol.com

twenty thousand troops sent from eight western nations. Increasingly, the
educated Chinese demanded the creation of a modern, republican form of
government.

JAPAN BEFORE WESTERN CONTACT

People migrating from Korea, Southeast Asia, and the South Pacific
eventually settled in the Japanese archipelago. During the Jōmon period
(1200–300 BCE), people lived in small settlements and grew rice.
They had limited use of metal but developed sophisticated pottery. The
Yayoi period (300 BCE–300 CE) followed with irrigated rice growing,
population increase, indigenous religion, and iron making. The Kofun
period (250–538 CE) is renowned for large key-shaped burial mounds,
called *kofun*. Also called the Yamato period, in this era powerful clans
and military chiefs governed. Exchanges developed with Korea and

China, and Chinese writing was imported in this period. In the Asuku era (538–710 CE) Buddhism arrived from China, coming through Korea. Japan sent students to China to study Buddhism and Confucianism. In 710 elite families on the island now known as Honshū established the first permanent capital with a stable bureaucratic government at Heijokyo (the city of Nara today), beginning the Nara era (710–94 CE).

Early Japan drew heavily on Chinese and Korean cultures. Nara was modeled after a Tang dynasty city and quickly grew to a population of two hundred thousand. The Nara era lasted only eighty years, but during this time Japanese elites, including the emperor and powerful nobles, significantly advanced and solidified Japanese civilization, strengthening the economy and public administration. They improved a network of roads that linked provincial towns to Nara, collected taxes efficiently, and minted coins. Buddhism took hold in Japan during this period after the emperor embraced and actively promoted it.

Factional fighting developed as imperial family members, leading court officials, and Buddhist priests contended for influence. Simultaneously, the central government's financial burdens grew faster than its tax revenue. As the court dismissed nonessential officials and allowed districts to create private militia forces, central authority weakened. In 794 new leaders took charge and moved the capital about 25 miles northwest to Heiankyo, or Heian (now called Kyōto).

After the capital was moved, imperial authority grew stronger. The emperor ruled under the Confucian Chinese "Mandate of Heaven" and was treated as a descendant of the Shintō Sun Goddess (see chapter 2). At first the Heian era (794–1185) continued Nara culture, and the city followed a Chinese layout, but the last mission to Tang China was in 838 and Chinese influence waned. Over time a sophisticated culture emerged in an insulated court society. At the height of the Heian era, a Japanese noblewoman, Murasaki Shikibu, wrote the world's first novel, *The Tale of Genji*.

The rich and remarkable Heian culture only lasted 150 years. Over time religious establishments sought titles for landed estates, tax waivers, and immunity from inspection. Land and people increasingly fell outside central government control and taxing authority. Although a highly artistic court culture flourished, political authority eroded. As central authority declined, military disturbances spread in outlying areas. Major court families began to attack one another, and the emperor, controlled by the Fujiwara noble family, became involved in the intrigue and conflict.

Eventually, the country's top military general, or shogun, rose to power. He created a new *de facto* capital 200 miles to the northeast in the city of Kamakura.

The Kamakura era (1185–1333) was a transition to Japan's "medieval" era. For the next six hundred years, the emperor and court remained in Kyōto, but they were weak and relegated to ceremonial functions. The *bushi*, or warrior class, held real power and controlled civil, military, and judicial matters. The shogun, leader of the *bushi* class, became the *de facto* national ruler. In this epoch the samurai (main warriors of the *bushi*) occupied center stage. They followed a code of conduct, the way of the warrior, *bushidō*, which emphasized extreme loyalty, mastery of martial arts, and honor to the death.

In this era Buddhism spread among the common people. Two Buddhist sects, Pure Land and Zen (discussed in chapter 2) became popular with the lower and middle classes. Zen appealed to the military class, merging the *bushidō* honor code with strict Zen religious discipline.

In the late Kamakura era, warring armies spread across Japan and aligned with powerful clans that struggled for political and military dominance. Japan's feudal era has interesting parallels to the European Middle Ages. Both had agricultural economies with land-based wealth; both had a powerful warrior class but a very weak centralized state; and both had a system of landholding lords who held the most power, exercised military rule, and required loyalty from many low-ranking vassals.

Although Japan had limited relations with China, some commercial and cultural contacts continued. In 1268 the Mongol-Yuan regime in Beijing demanded tribute from Japan. Japan's emperor rebuffed the demands from distant China. Outraged, China sent a large military force to subdue small, insolent Japan. In the first Mongol invasion (1274), China sent six hundred ships with twenty-three thousand troops. A sudden typhoon decimated the Mongol forces while they were at sea. In 1291 they returned in a second invasion attempt. After weeks of fighting, another typhoon struck. It again destroyed the Chinese-Mongol fleet. The Japanese interpreted their victory as due to supernatural intervention and believed a divine wind, or *kamikaze*, had saved them.

After the Kamakura era, power moved back to Kyōto. In the Muromachi era (1337–1573) trade with China resumed. Several leaders attempted to unify the country but without success, so internal warfare continued. Eventually, a major civil conflict, the Ōnin War (1467–77),

Figure 1.3. Hideyoshi's castle in Osaka (Author photo).

devastated Kyōto and effectively ended its national authority. Decades of almost continuous chaos, anarchy, and strife followed. Peasants rebelled against their landlords, and samurai deserted their military lords. Central government control ceased, and the imperial court became impoverished. Provincial domains emerged after the Ōnin War, but they were small. Many arose from among the samurai who had overthrown their lords. As warfare became endemic, fortified castle towns dotted the landscape (as also occurred in feudal Europe).

During this era Europeans reached Japan. About thirty years after they arrived in China, the Portuguese landed on the southern island of Kyūshū in 1543. The Spanish followed in 1587. Next came the Dutch in 1609, followed by the British in 1613. Some Japanese began to study European civilization, and trade grew. The Europeans traded firearms, fabrics, glassware, clocks, tobacco, and other western innovations for Japanese gold and silver. European firearms made warfare in Japan more deadly. A few powerful military leaders arose to defeat the competing warlords. Slowly these leaders consolidated their power and began to unify Japan.

Eventually, the military leader Toyotomi Hideyoshi (1537–1598, Toyotomi is the family name) gained control, unified the country, and constructed a major castle in Ōsaka. He built a new national government structure, distributed territory, and created new systems of land measurement and tax assessment. Hideyoshi's major ambition was to conquer China. In 1592 he invaded Korea with two hundred thousand troops. At the time Korea was sovereign but paid tribute to China. Hideyoshi's armies quickly overran the Korean peninsula but were ultimately defeated by a combined Korean-Chinese force. In 1597 Hideyoshi launched a second invasion, but it abruptly halted with his death in 1598, ending, for three hundred years, Japan's attempt to extend itself into Korea.

A new leader, Tokugawa Ieyasu, (1543–1616) benefited from Hideyoshi's achievements. Already a powerful general, Hideyoshi had given Ieyasu the agriculturally rich Kantō region (a flat area of central Japan around Tōkyō) in 1590 as a reward for help in suppressing a rebellious clan. At Edo (meaning "bay entrance," later renamed Tōkyō) the Tokugawa clan maintained huge estates and built a new headquarters. After Hideyoshi's death, Tokugawa Ieyasu seized control to become the shogun. He conquered enemies, redistributed the spoils of war to allies, and established a new system of central authority. The weak, figurehead emperor remained in Kyōto. Real national power was located in Edo. The Tokugawa era (1603–1868), in which Ieyasu and his descendants occupied the shogunate, brought over 250 years of peace, prosperity, and stability.

At first, trade with foreigners was limited, but it soon grew. The shoguns disliked both the flow of new foreign goods outside their control and foreigners, especially Christian missionaries. They feared a loss of obedience from local lords who converted to the foreign religion. In 1612 Ieyasu ordered his retainers to reject Christianity. Restrictions soon intensified, and by 1622 the shogunate was having missionaries executed. In 1624 the shogunate expelled the Spanish and their missionaries, and five years later it executed thousands of Japanese Christians in an attempt to eradicate the foreign religion. By 1635 the Tokugawa regime had closed Japan to the outside world. The regime only permitted restricted and tightly controlled trade with the Dutch in the remote southern port of Nagasaki. The shogun forbade the Japanese from traveling outside Japan, on penalty of death.

The Tokugawa regime reorganized Japanese society along Confucian principles. At the top was the powerless, ceremonial emperor in Kyōto. Next were the shogun and samurai who held real political and economic power. In descending hierarchical order were peasants, artisans, and merchants. Finally at the very bottom were the *eta*, Japan's "untouchable" caste, considered barely human. In the Tokugawa era trade, craft production, and even small-scale manufacturing greatly increased. Cities grew. By the mid-1700s, Edo had over one million residents, making it the world's largest city.

Strong central authority and rule by the shogun reduced internal conflict. Japan was organized into 250 to 260 territories, or *han*, each ruled by a local lord, or daimyo. To maintain control, the shogun created an "alternate attendance system." In order to prevent revolt, daimyos were required to spend every other year in residence in Edo and to leave family members in Edo as hostages after they returned to their *han*.

Over time, the Tokugawa warrior-agrarian system ceased to align with an emergent, vibrant, urban society dominated by merchants and expanding trade. Rule was by a large government bureaucracy staffed by many samurai who received a stipend but no longer fought. The samurai functioned more as bureaucrats than as warriors, and they increasingly lacked clear purpose or direction. Compounding this situation, Japan's population grew significantly in the era of peace, prosperity, artistic development, and technological improvement.

Meanwhile, European ships were scouting Japan's coasts seeking entry. Each time the Japanese drove them off. By the mid-1800s, the United States was expanding its influence into the Pacific. Well behind the Europeans who controlled much of China, the United States sought relations with Japan in 1846 but was turned away. However, in 1856 Commodore Matthew C. Perry's large squadron of gunships (called "black ships") sailed into Edo Bay, changing everything. The United States opened Japan to outsiders, literally at gunpoint, ending 250 years of self-imposed isolation and triggering a dramatic transformation of Japanese society.

KOREA BEFORE JAPANESE CONTROL

Korea's first kingdom—Gojoseon—appeared about 700 BCE. After about three hundred years, the capital moved to Pyongyang (today's North Korean capital). During a coup in 194 BCE, the Gojoseon king fled to Manchuria, and China (then the Han dynasty) entered to subdue Korea. China divided Korea into several small, weak states, which evolved into four kingdoms. One (Silla) soon defeated a small neighbor (Kaya). This began the seven-hundred-year Three Kingdoms era (57 BCE–668 CE) of Goguryeo (also spelled Koguryŏ), Baekje (also spelled Paekche), and Silla.

Map 1.4. Three Kingdom's Korea. Source:
http://commons.wikimedia.org/wiki/File:Three_
Kingdoms_of_Korea_Map.png.

During the Three Kingdoms era, Chinese influence spread and Buddhism was introduced. The kingdoms periodically fought wars against one another and formed alliances with or against the Chinese. In 660 CE, Silla allied with China to overthrow the other two kingdoms. Silla then drove the Chinese (at that time the Tang dynasty) forces out of Korea. By 676, Silla had unified Korea. Korean civilization greatly advanced for 300 years under the Silla kingdom. Buddhism became the official state religion. Eventually, warlords to the north amassed enough power to overtake Korea. They founded a new kingdom, Goryeo (also written as Koryŏ, the origin of the English word Korea). The Goryeo kingdom (918–1392), faced internal and external threats. In 1231 the Mongols invaded Korea, forcing the royal family to flee. For the next 150 years, the Mongols had great control over Korea.

In 1392 General Yi broke free to establish the Joseon (also written Chosŏn and called Yi) dynasty (1392–1910). He moved the capital to Hanyang (modern-day Seoul). By 1394 Buddhism had waned and General

Yi reorganized Korean society along neo-Confucian principles and made many cultural improvements. King Sejong, the fourth monarch of the Yi era, devised a new, simple writing system (*hangul*). Until that time, all writing was in difficult to learn Chinese characters. *Hangul* had an alphabet based on sounds and allowed literacy to spread to more Koreans. Koreans continue to use *hangul* and regard it as a source of great pride.

As you read earlier, in 1592 and 1598, Toyotomi Hideyoshi invaded Korea on his way to China, causing great devastation on the peninsula. After Hideyoshi left, and as the Koreans were rebuilding, the Manchus invaded in the 1620s and 1630s. The Korean kingdom moved toward a strict isolationist policy and barred all foreign contact. The Yi dynasty earned the foreign nickname "Hermit Kingdom" because of its attempt to protect Korea from western imperialism, already evident in China. By the late 1800s, Russia was pushing toward Korea from the west and north, and modernizing Japan to the east was eying it. Eventually, the Japanese, not the westerners, colonized Korea.

THE RISE OF IMPERIAL JAPAN

Japan managed to avoid the encroaching western powers until the mid-1800s. In its early history, Japan had borrowed heavily from China but then isolated itself for centuries. During the Tokugawa era, a complex, prosperous society emerged with a landed aristocracy, samurai, peasants, merchants, and castles. A distinct, sophisticated culture arose in large cities and small market towns.

Once the United States forced Japan to open, the Japanese quickly adapted. In just fifty years, Japan went from an isolated, quasi-feudal society of sword-carrying samurai to an emerging industrial power. Perhaps you have seen the 2003 Tom Cruise film *The Last Samurai* Although it plays loose with historical facts, the plot centers on an actual fight over abolishing Japan's traditional society.

Japan was remarkable, both as the first nonwestern country to industrialize and for the speed of its modernization. It was soon mimicking other imperial powers by going to war, first with China in the Sino-Japanese War (1894–95) and then with Russia in the Russo-Japanese War (1904–05). Each time it won and gained territory.

How did Japan transform itself so quickly? In simple terms, a critical faction of the elite class came to believe that unless Japan overturned its old feudal order and embraced western technological skills and knowledge, it would suffer China's humiliating fate. In a very clever strategy, members of this elite faction used a new boy emperor, Meiji, as a symbol to spearhead a new, vibrant Japan. In the name of the emperor, they actively borrowed western ideas, technologies, and organizational forms to remake Japan into a modern society. They sought to preserve Japan's independence and cultural core while beginning a dramatic era of transformation and modernization, the Meiji era (1868–1912).

Japan soon acquired colonies: Formosa (present-day Taiwan) in 1895 and Korea in 1910. When Korean nationalists fought back, Japan treated them harshly. They forced Koreans to learn Japanese and sent millions to work in Japanese mines or factories for very low wages. After Emperor Meiji died in 1912, a weak emperor (Taishō) assumed power. Japan faced a series of rebuffs: western nations rejected its plea for a racial equality clause at the 1919 Peace Conference after the First World War, the United States restricted Japanese immigration, and an international conference demanded reductions in Japan's navy. During the 1920s, Japan suffered a horrific earthquake, Emperor Taishō died, and the economy was in turmoil. Early in the 1930s, right-wing leaders gained control of the government. They assassinated political opponents, imposed censorship in education and the media, and built the military.

Japan's leaders ended democratic freedoms and sought expansion. First, they moved into Manchuria (1931) and then invaded China (1937). Japan allied with Nazi Germany and signed a 1936 Anti-Comintern Pact, against the Communist International (i.e., the Comintern) and the Soviet Union. Japan's invasion of China started the Pacific War almost five years before the attack on Pearl Harbor. China had become an independent republic in 1912, but it remained politically divided, militarily weak, and economically underdeveloped. While all wars are brutal, Japan's treatment of Chinese civilians, particularly in 1937 in Nanjing, was especially horrific. By 1941 Japan had spread across Pacific Asia, only to face defeat from the superior military power and atomic bomb of the United States in 1945.

In 1945 China emerged devastated and sharply divided. The nationalists (Kuomintang [KMT], also written Guomindang), led by Chang Kai-shek, held official power but had been intermittently fighting the Chinese Communist Party (CCP), under Mao Zedong, since the 1920s. After the Japanese left, the KMT and communists engaged in a civil war. In 1949 Mao won and declared a new government, the People's Republic of China (PRC). The defeated KMT fled to Taiwan with what remained of its army. It vowed to keep fighting mainland China. Half a million KMT soldiers and two million refugees overran the small island of Taiwan, once part of China and later a Japanese colony. They took control and arrested or executed native Taiwanese who objected. The PRC limited contact with western countries but accepted military and industrial aid from the Soviet Union until about 1960. This self-imposed era of isolation continued until the 1972 visit by U.S. President Richard Nixon.

AFTER THE PACIFIC WAR

Americans tend to see the Second World War as a series of battles across the Pacific ending with the atomic bombings of Hiroshima and Nagasaki. However, the war greatly affected the entire region. In 1946 nearly all factories, railroads, ports, and roads in Japan, China, Taiwan, and Korea were damaged. Cities lay in rubble. Millions of unemployed, dislocated, hungry, and homeless people filled the streets and wandered the countryside. The contrast with the world's first modern superpower, the United States, could not have been starker. Despite many deaths, the United States lost a only tiny percentage of its population and none of its cities was bombed or invaded. It had greatly expanded and upgraded its massive industrial and agricultural base during wartime.

Today we recognize two Koreas, North and South. For thousands of years, Korea was one country with a distinct language and culture. After Japan's defeat, the Soviet Union created a zone of occupation in the north when anti-Japanese guerrilla fighters came out of hiding. The Soviets and Chinese Communists supported these ex-guerrilla leaders, including Kim Il-sung (1912–94). In the south, the United States also set up a zone of occupation and sought to prevent a communist takeover. Unable to agree, the two major powers divided Korea along the Thirty-Eighth parallel.

In the south a new Korean National Assembly elected Syngman Rhee as president. Rhee was an anti-communist Christian who had been educated in the United States. Backed by the United States, Rhee welcomed many businesspeople who had collaborated with the Japanese colonial regime. As occurred in Germany, Cold War alignments divided Korea. After rising tensions, in 1950 the north, led by Kim Il-sung, invaded the south. During the three-year Korean War, five million people died, over half of them civilians (about 10 percent of Korea's prewar population). It ended in a military stalemate with a return to the Thirty-Eighth parallel.

During the sixty years since division, South Korea retained close ties to the United States and built a powerful capitalist, industrial economy.

Between the Korean War truce in 1953 and the mid-1980s, nondemocratic military-based leaders ruled South Korea. Yet they created a strong economy by the mid-1970s. After mass civilian unrest in the 1980s, a modern and open democratic society emerged. Kim Il-sung continued to rule North Korea until his death in 1994. He converted Communist rule into an extreme system of total self-reliance, *juche*. Today North Korea remains an isolated, impoverished country under an extremely repressive regime.

In the minds of many, there are also two Chinas. From the PRC victory (1949) through Mao Zedong's death (1976), China advanced, but it also experienced several major setbacks. Two especially harsh times were the Great Leap Forward (1958–63) and the Cultural Revolution (1966–76). The Great Leap Forward, with agricultural collectivization of one hundred million people and promotion of "backyard" furnaces with an expectation that peasants could produce high-quality steel, had disastrous consequences. It produced crop failures, unusable products, and mass famine with as many as thirty million people starving to death. The Cultural Revolution advanced extreme ideological purity. Radical teenage Red Guards spurred on by Mao, attacked all old or western-related ideas or objects. They tormented, beat, or killed teachers, doctors, writers, and scientists. Universities closed, and all scientific, intellectual, artistic, and refined cultural life in China stopped for a decade.

When Mao Zedong died in 1976, China was still an underdeveloped country. Mao's successors, especially Deng Xiaoping, introduced dramatic economic reforms and opened China's economy to the outside world by 1980. This transformed China into the world's fastest-growing industrializing country. Despite rising incomes and technological advances, the one-party government continued to squash attempts to democratize politics and expand free expression. This was evident in the bloody suppression of the 1989 pro-democracy movement known in China as the June Fourth Incident and elsewhere as the Tiananmen Square protests.

Taiwan followed a path similar to that of South Korea. The KMT established a harsh dictatorship, but by the 1960s–70s, with the United States providing military protection from the PRC, the economy grew. By the 1980s, rule by the KMT nationalists had weakened. After the lifting of martial law in 1987, a pro-democracy movement emerged. Today Taiwan is a highly industrialized, democratic society.

With its defeat in 1945, Japan was reduced to rubble. From 1945 to 1952, the United States occupied and guided the country. Japan's second rapid rise to a world industrial power in the 1960s–80s was cited as an "economic miracle." Its fast-rising boom or "bubble economy" crashed in 1990. Fifteen economic years of stagnation followed.

Today, with democratization and rapid economic growth, South Korea and Taiwan are vibrant, modern, politically open societies. "Market socialism" has reshaped China's economy. In late 2010 China displaced Japan as the world's second-largest economy. Japan continues to face a slow economic decline and lack of direction. North Korea remains an isolated, impoverished country under strict military rule.

CONCLUSION

Summarizing East Asia's long, complex history is not easy. The five present countries have traded and interacted with each other for thousands of years. Until western entry in the 1500s, East Asians had little direct contact with European-Mediterranean civilization. Over the centuries, East and West developed distinct worldviews, some of which persist to this day. For centuries China was a dominant cultural force in the region. China's political instability, internal divisions, and humiliating exploitation by foreigners made Japan want to avoid its fate. Japan and Korea experienced centuries of internal warfare but periods of great advancement as well. Each sought to protect and nurture a distinct culture and way of life. East Asia's history has consequences today, both in shared cultural values and themes (see chapter 2) and in lingering antagonisms among East Asian nations (discussed in chapter 6).

2

EAST ASIAN CULTURE

You know the word *"culture,"* but it is a complex idea. You learned your own culture as a child, absorbed it with little conscious awareness, and see it as "normal life." You are so close to it that it is invisible, like the water in which a fish swims. Learning about a different culture, such as that of East Asia, makes culture more visible. Culture explains why you see certain behaviors and beliefs as normal and proper but others as odd, unusual, or strange. You share culture with many people, such as an entire nation, but also carry your culture internally as an individual. Culture includes both familiar physical objects (e.g., the Statue of Liberty, cell phones, baseball caps, and McDonalds) and feelings, beliefs, customs, tastes, and values. Cultural parts fit together and mutually reinforce one another, forming cultural systems.

THE WAYS OF CULTURE

In this chapter you will learn about East Asian culture. We start by looking at five ways in which culture influences a person's life: worldview, morality, expression, identity, and daily practice.

Culture as Worldview

Culture shapes how you think, see the world, and organize knowledge. It provides assumptions about the world, (e.g., what is human nature, can you trust other people?). Since the ancient Greeks, western culture has emphasized individual action or independent agency. Its worldview praises individual initiative, personal freedom, and rational thinking. It puts at center stage the lone hero who competes and achieves. By contrast an East Asian worldview emphasizes collective action, group harmony, and cooperation. It focuses on connecting with other people and maintaining a balance of relations within a group. In it the individual is part of a group and defined largely by his or her relationships within a web of others. These are the broad trends, and every culture has its exceptions.[1]

Culture as a Source of Morality

Culture defines what is proper or improper, right or wrong. This takes many forms, such as "wise sayings," well-known folktales, religious beliefs, and other strongly held values. Culture's moral underpinnings are why cultural misunderstandings so quickly develop into intense disagreements when people of different cultures come into contact. We can trace American ideas about morality back to Western European thinking, and further back to the ancient Greeks. The Roman republic and early Christian Church incorporated many Greek ideas about individual moral responsibility and justice. Judeo-Christian beliefs about obeying God's laws also shaped western moral thinking. As you saw in the last chapter on history, competing value traditions, historical events, and struggles over many centuries shaped East Asian culture, and beliefs regarding morality arose from a confluence of diverse religious and nonreligious sources.

Culture as Mode of Expression

Culture shapes how people speak, write, and express themselves, including language, nonverbal gestures, literature, art, music, and ideals of modesty and beauty. Cultural "scripts" tell people whether eye contact, a bow, or a hand gesture is appropriate. To take one example, your culture has taught you to hear certain sounds or musical tones as pleasant and others as irritating noise. Culture also defines musical instruments (piano or violin vs. flute or Japanese koto or Chinese erhu) and forms of writing.

Culture as Identity

Culture reinforces feelings of national pride and shared identity, that is, who we are as a people. It blends ideas of race, ethnicity, origin, and unity. Americans view themselves as a "new nation" and a melting pot of immigrants because all but native Amerindian people and African slaves migrated from "the old country." By contrast immigration is relatively rare in East Asia. Many people proudly trace their civilization, heritage, and ancestors back thousands of years. Part of an American identity is never having been conquered by another nation. By contrast foreigners periodically conquered China and Korea, China and Japan experienced years of western domination, and Korea faced incursions by both Japan and westerners.

Lady playing Japanese koto

Writing

Hello, how are you today? (English)

こんにちは, 今日は元気ですか? (Japanese)

안녕하세요, 오늘은 얼마나? (Korean)

你好, 你今天好嗎? (Chinese)

Chinese erhu

Figure 2.1. Forms of writing and musical instruments: Koto, Erhu. Source: http://commons.wikimedia.org/wiki/File:Lady_playing_koto.jpg and http://commons.wikimedia.org/wiki/File:Erhu.png.

Culture as Daily Practice

We express our culture through clothing styles, foods, sports, holidays, and daily activities. For example, you may give gifts, yet the expectations of when and to whom to give a gift, whether you must wrap it, and appropriate types of gifts vary by culture, and differ between East Asia and the United States. Culture shapes the annual cycle of holidays by which we collectively recognize significant events. Americans recognize major Christian holidays (e.g., Christmas, Easter) and national holidays (Independence Day, Labor Day, Memorial Day, Thanksgiving). Few East Asians celebrate Christmas or the other U.S. holidays.[2] China's biggest holiday is the lunar New Year, which usually occurs in early February. People celebrate it with fireworks, special foods, and family visits. Japan's big holidays are the New Year, celebrated on January 1–3, and "Golden Week," a series of holidays in early May. In addition to the lunar New Year, Koreans celebrate *chuseok* on the fifteenth day of the eighth lunar month, usually in September. They gather as families, eat special foods, and give thanks to ancestors.[3]

Family gatherings to honor ancestors are common across East Asia. In Japan millions return to their hometowns each fifteenth day of the seventh lunar month (early August) for *obon*, a Buddhist festival that honors departed ancestors with special foods and dancing. Many in China and Taiwan celebrate a ghost or spirit holiday at the same time and burn fake paper money to help the souls of the departed.

Each East Asian society has distinct customs and daily practices, such as removing shoes or bowing. Westerners tend to drink coffee or soft drinks, eat potatoes, and use forks, while East Asians tend to drink tea and eat rice with chopsticks. However, such differences have blurred in recent decades, and the type of tea and style of chopstick vary by Asian society. In Japan people politely form lines and wait quietly. In China people might break into line and raise voices, and the Chinese and Koreans generally speak louder than the Japanese do. East Asia is famous for its martial arts, but kung fu comes from China, judo and karate from Japan, and tae kwon do from Korea. Interest in western sports varies, with baseball and soccer popular in Japan, basketball popular in China, and soccer popular in the Koreas.

THREE TRAITS OF CULTURE

Culture is not a single, static thing but has three main traits: fluidity, layers, and diversity. Culture constantly develops and changes. Some parts change little across the generations, but other parts are very dynamic. Ancient traditions and contemporary trends comingle. Cultural ideas and styles also spill across national borders. Aspects of western culture flow into East Asia, and you may discover aspects of East Asian culture within your society.

Cultures have layers, from low to high. You may have heard someone called "cultured." This refers to a person familiar with the upper layer of refined, highbrow, or high culture. The primary consumers of this level are members of society's sophisticated, well-educated, upper social class. Most lower- and middle-income people primarily encounter high culture in school. Examples of high culture in the United States include knowing certain authors, such as Shakespeare, Hemingway, or Thoreau; being familiar with the fine arts, such as paintings by Monet or Picasso; and attending classical music, ballet, or dramatic theater. High culture extends to leisure activities (e.g., yacht sailing, opera), specific kinds of clothing (e.g., tuxedos, evening gowns), and certain foods (e.g., caviar, snails). Most people of modest incomes and education participate exclusively or usually in "popular culture." This is the world of television, hit movies, video games, and tracking celebrities. Popular culture involves mass spectator sports (e.g., baseball, football, auto racing); popular music (rock, Top 40, hip-hop, country); wearing jeans, t-shirts, or tank-tops; and eating "fast food."

East Asia also has cultural layers. Attend a high-culture formal event in Japan and women may wear an elegant kimono, in Korean a fancy hanbok, and in China or Taiwan a cheongsam. Attend a popular culture event like a baseball game and people will dress in jeans, t-shirts, and sneakers as in the United States.

Societies vary with regard to diversity. Some are multicultural, that is, a mix of several cultures in one society. Culture can refer both to the dominant or mainstream culture of an entire society and to the beliefs and practices of a society's subgroups. The United States has many subgroups—by region, city or rural area, generation, religion, social class, and racial or ethnic group—each with a distinct culture or subculture. East Asian societies also vary. China is diverse, with many minority subgroups that vary by region, language, religion, and ethnicity, while South Korea is more uniform. Japan is mostly uniform, like South Korea, but has growing minority populations (diversity is further discussed in chapter 5).

IS THERE AN EAST ASIAN CULTURE?

Each East Asian society has its national culture, cultural layers, and subculture mix. You might ask, is there a single East Asian culture? In some respects, the answer is no: there are multiple cultural traditions, customs, and ways of life. In other respects, it is yes: some traditions, values, and outlooks are shared across East Asia. It is a matter of degree more than a yes or no issue. Despite lacking a common language or government and having very different national traditions, East Asians share many similar views and cultural characteristics. This is because the past profoundly shapes today's culture.

American culture developed as European settlers arrived roughly four hundred years ago. They encountered and conquered Amerindians then spread across a vast, rich land, bringing a language and legal system from Britain, European civilization and customs, Judeo-Christian religious beliefs, and Africans as slaves. East Asia's history differs significantly. For over two thousand years, China's powerful, advanced civilization shaped the region's culture.

China (Sino) Civilization and Confucius

China is the major source of shared East Asian culture. Chinese-origin principles of government, family, and even daily practices, like using chopsticks, spread across East Asia. Many Chinese principles originated with Confucius. He was a real person, Kong Qiu, who lived in China about 500 BCE— five centuries prior to Christianity. His system of ideas, Confucianism, is less a religion than a set of ethical principles and cultivated habits that guide the organization of government, community affairs, and social relations. Included in Confucianism are assumptions about human nature, good and evil, and life's priorities. Confucianism spread across the region unevenly, and rose or fell from favor over time, and it remained unknown outside of East Asia for two thousand years.[4]

Figure 2.2. Confucius. Source: http://commons. wikimedia.org/wiki/File:Konfuzius-1770.jpg.

Five Principles of Confucianism

A useful way to grasp Confucianism is to consider its five basic principles: Humanity, Ritual, Relationships, Loyalty and Being a Gentleman. As with any set of principles derived from a moral-value system, people's actual behaviors often fail to match the ideals.

Humanity. Confucius emphasized the ethic of reciprocity. It is a version of the West's Golden Rule: treat others as you wish others to treat you. He saw each of us as born with intrinsic similarities and potential goodness, not in original sin. Focusing on this life, he said we can better ourselves with study, practice, and self-cultivation. This idea continues today with a great interest in self-improvement across East Asia. Confucius also demanded humane behavior and deference. We demonstrate our humanity every day by showing respect for others, including their place in society.

Ritual. Rituals are the set routines that people follow in ceremonies and daily life. For many westerners in recent decades, ritual has acquired a negative connotation and implies going through empty, formal motions. In Confucian societies, few rituals are ossified, empty practices. Instead, aligned with the idea of propriety, rituals are repeated attitudes, habits, and daily actions that guide one to proper conduct. By cultivating and following proper rituals, individuals are able to create a stable, harmonious society of contented, cooperating people. Rituals help to internalize and coordinate behavior by reinforcing preferred forms of social interaction: quietly reflecting before acting, remaining calm and polite, practicing humility and propriety, and sustaining mutual respect and harmony. This contrasts with the high value western culture places on thinking independently, making autonomous choices, and seeking personal satisfaction.

Relationships. Human relationships are central in all cultures but profoundly emphasized in Confucianism. Each of us is part of a relationship with others: as child to parents, as elder brother/sister to younger siblings, as a teammate, and so on. Relationships define our duties, responsibilities, and expected behaviors. Confucius saw all relationships ordered into a vast system. To him sustaining a healthy, harmonious society essentially depends on each of us recognizing our place in relationships and accepting the responsibilities and obligations that come with that place.

Loyalty. Being loyal is a great human virtue and an extension of our obligations to family, spouse, friends, community, and nation/government. Loyalty spreads outward—to family, a spouse, friends, community, and the ruler. Relationships define to whom we owe loyalty. Filial piety is a special virtue flowing from loyalty. It is a child's obligation to respect his or her parents (this idea is explained in chapter 3).

Western culture tends to elevate loyalty to oneself, not to others (e.g., be true to yourself), and it encourages us to seek personal satisfaction, or perhaps romantic love with one other person. In contrast traditional Confucian culture places loyalty to family, not to oneself, first. Confucianism considers the emphasis on pursuing personal ambitions and desires to be selfish, unrefined, and immature.

Being a Gentleman. Confucianism admonishes us to strive to become a "gentleman." To put it in different terms, we should strive to combine the ideals of moral guide and wise, humble scholar. As Confucian teaching spread across East Asia and received government support, it came to be believed that the ideal person is highly moral; respects enduring values; studies broadly in the arts, humanities, and sciences; exhibits filial piety; acts benevolently; and, most of all, engages in continuous self-cultivation. Its opposite is an ill informed, superficial, hedonistic, and materialistic person always bragging and chasing after the latest fads.

Applied to daily life, Confucianism tells us to study hard, respect our elders and teachers, and serve the community. Ancient China created an examination system, with examinations based on knowing the Confucian classics. All who passed the difficult examination brought honor and prestige to their families and communities. They could advance to the higher calling of serving society and the emperor, who communicated with the heavens and possessed spiritual powers (the examination system is discussed in chapter 4).

Confucianism is the origin of many East Asian cultural ideals, such as humility, frugality, patience, self-discipline, dedication, and respect for learning. It encourages constant self-improvement, obedience to authority, harmony over conflict, and deference to elders. Like any complex belief system, Confucianism has positive and negative sides. Obedience and loyalty can reinforce strong work groups or contribute to cronyism. Strong families can cultivate affectionate relationships or enforce patriarchal domination. Group harmony can promote cooperative teamwork or stifle dissent, dampen creativity, and impose conformity. Observers have blamed Confucianism for encouraging authoritarian rulers, suppressing political dissent, and slowing social and economic development, and praised it for fostering diligence, social stability, and economic success.[5]

Centuries after Confucius died, Neo-Confucian movements arose in China, Japan and Korea. They revived select Confucian principles and were often stricter than original Confucianism, or blended Confucian elements with other beliefs, such as Daoism or Buddhism, which we examine next.

DAOISM

Like Confucianism, Daoism (also written Taoism) originated in China centuries before the Christian era and diffused across East Asia. It supposedly began with a real person (Laozi, also written Lao Tsu). Daoism is both a philosophy and a set of religious ideas; it focuses on the relationship between human beings and the natural environment. Daoism urges us to observe, understand, respect, and act in accordance with the forces of nature. It notes that natural forces operate in our daily lives, the heavens, and the physical world, and says it is unwise for humans to interfere with or resist such forces. Rather than trying to impose the human will onto society or nature, Daoism advises us to observe and listen very carefully to nature so we can adapt ourselves to its ways.[6]

The word *Dao* means "the way" or "the path." Daoism provides a pathway for living. It advises us to be adaptable, nonjudgmental, and flexible. The way of Daoism is to empty our minds and lives of clutter. This will enable us to be fully open to recognize, appreciate, and absorb the beauties and harmonies in nature. By becoming receptive, detached, and passive, we can better act spontaneously in accordance with nature. The phrase "go with the flow" expresses Daoist thinking. It implies accepting events as they come and aligning with the natural forces of the cosmos. Daoism advises placing mind and body in balance, as illustrated in the principles of yin and yang.

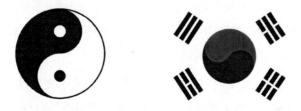

Figure 2.3. The Daoist symbols yin and yang. Among other places, they are found on the South Korean flag. Source: http://commons.wikimedia.org/wiki/File:Esoteric_Taijitu.svg and http://commons.wikimedia.org/wiki/File:Flag_of_South_Korea.svg.

Aspects of life that Westerners see as being opposites—mind and body, emotion and reason, thought and action, hot and cold, male and female, strong and weak—the Daoist views as two complementary sides of a unified whole. A central idea is *qi* (also written *chi*, or *ki*). Often translated as "energy force," *qi* is an intangible, natural, vital energy field. It emanates from everything in the universe. *Qi* includes the movement and quality of the air that circulates around us, the earth's magnetic field, the moon's gravitational pull, cosmic radiation, sunlight, color vibrations, and flows of thoughts and emotions. Many East Asian medical practices, such as acupuncture, and the martial arts attempt to channel and harness flows of *qi*. *Qi* flows within each of us. Vibrant, freely flowing *qi* promotes strength, energy, happiness, and health. Blocked *qi* makes us weak, physically sick, and emotionally distraught.

BUDDHISM

Confucianism and Daoism influenced East Asian culture and provided moral guidance, but they are not universally considered to be religions. The Judeo-Christian religious beliefs that shaped American views on morality had little impact in East Asia. After three centuries of Christian missionary work, only a tiny percentage of people in China, Japan, or Taiwan are Christians. South Korea is the exception, with nearly 30 percent of Koreans practicing Christianity, primarily Protestant faiths.[7]

The most widely practiced religion in East Asia, Buddhism also shaped East Asian beliefs and morality. It spread from India to China and then to the rest of Asia. It began with a real person, Siddhartha Gotama, over five hundred years before Jesus Christ in what is today Nepal.

Buddhism asserts that this life is full of suffering. To end it we must abandon attachments to material possessions and show compassion toward all living things.

THE FOUR NOBLE TRUTHS OF BUDDHISM

1. Life is filled with suffering

2. Craving, desire and attachments are the cause of suffering.

3. Suffering ends when attachments and craving cease.

4. Freedom from suffering comes from living by principles of the Buddha (eightfold path) including mediation, self-discipline, kindness, and good conduct.

Figure 2.4. Buddha statue in Kamakura. Source: http://commons.
wikimedia.org/wiki/File:KamakuraDaibutsu4049.jpg.

Buddhism, like many religions, has several branches. Its three
major branches are Theravāda (Teaching of the Elders), Mahāyāna (The
Great Vehicle), and Vajrayāna (which includes the Tibetan and Japanese
Shingon schools). Each branch emphasizes certain Buddhist teachings and
prevails in different parts in Asia: Theravāda in South and Southeast Asia;
Mahāyāna in China, Japan, and Korea; and Vajrayāna in Tibet.

Mahāyāna, the dominant East Asian branch, emerged around 100 CE
as an open, accessible interpretation of Buddhist teachings. It emphasizes
the inclusion of everyone, not just monks, and teaches that laypeople can
attain enlightenment (blissful spiritual transcendence, also called nirvana)
in a lifetime. Mahāyāna Buddhism has many schools; westerners are most
likely to know of the Zen school (called Chan in Chinese, Seon in Korea).
It started in China from cross-fertilization with Daoism about 500 CE.
Zen greatly influenced Japanese culture through the *bushidō* (way of the
warrior), tea ceremony, and artistic principles.

Three other major Mahāyāna schools include Tendai, Pure Land, and
Nichiren. Tendai (Tien Tai in pinyin Chinese) focuses on one Buddhist
teaching, the Lotus Sutra. It incorporates other beliefs, including Japan's
indigenous religion, Shintō. Pure Land Buddhism spread throughout
China, Japan, Korea, and Taiwan. It advises kindness, moral living, and
meditation to reach a "pure land" that is close to final enlightenment,
somewhat similar to the Christian idea of heaven. Nichiren Buddhism

began with a Japanese monk in the 1200s. It emphasizes repeatedly reciting mantras and chanting.

Buddhism differs from the Abrahamic religious traditions of Judaism, Christianity, and Islam. It has no one holy book or belief in a single, all-powerful God who sends humans laws, like the Ten Commandants. Nor is Buddhism exclusive. Rather, it is syncretic, (i.e., it combines different beliefs and merges disparate traditions) and assumes there is an underlying unity. Thus, a person can be Buddhist and accept other religions as well. Syncretism encourages flexibility and a blending of other religious beliefs, such as shamanism and Shintō (discussed in next section). Besides advising compassion and guiding daily living, Buddhism advises us to care for the souls of the departed. In Japan, Korea, and Taiwan, even nondevout Buddhists will have Buddhist funerals, cemeteries, and prayers for ancestors.

GHOSTS, ORACLES, SHAMANISM, AND SHINTŌ

East Asia is home to many local religions that influence its culture. In addition to a Muslim population, China has many local folk religions in which the line between sacred and secular blurs, as does the line between this world and an invisible world of gods, ghosts, and spirits. Practices around temple and home rituals are a mixture of ancestor worship, animism, popular Daoist and Buddhist beliefs, and Confucian ethics. People will carry lucky charms, consult oracles, and burn fake money to help the deceased in the spirit world. Shamanism is practiced in much of Korea. A shaman is someone who can communicate with the spirit world to find cures, fight evils, or learn fortunes.

Shintō, Japan's national religion, is so deeply integrated into Japanese culture that it is difficult to separate it from general cultural beliefs and practices. Shintō lacks a founding person or single sacred text. Instead of a single god, it has thousands of *kami* or spirit forces. *Kami* can intervene in daily human affairs, assisting or thwarting people. Japan's emperor is Shintō's spiritual head and traces his descent to an all-powerful sun goddess, Amaterasu. The emperor's historical connections with Shintō ended with the signing of Japan's Peace Constitution in 1946, which legally separated government from religion. Until the end of the Second World War, many in Japan treated the emperor as a living god.

Daoism and Shintō differ in origins and beliefs, yet both share a great respect for natural forces and try to harmonize humans with nature. In Shintō *kami* can be a magnificent waterfall or mountain, a thunderstorm, or the beauty of a sunset or rock formation. Very few Japanese see themselves as being religious, but most follow minor Shintō practices in daily life for good luck and enjoy many Shintō community celebrations.

OTHER CULTURAL PRACTICES

Besides the major traditions of Confucianism, Daoism, and Buddhism, East Asian cultures encourage other daily beliefs: a belief in "face," adopting a long-term perspective, and respect for status. You may have heard of "face saving" or "losing face." *Face* means reputation or prestige and honor in the eyes of others. The idea of face exists in western cultures, but a strong sense of face is pervasive across East Asia. The cultural belief of living in a web of interconnections with others means that your face, or reputation, as an honorable and upstanding person extends to your family, ancestors, community, school, and workplace. People feel pressure to uphold face and avoid bringing dishonor to self, family, and community. When interacting with a social superior or equal, you do not want to put him or her in a situation of losing face.[8]

Adopting a long-term perspective may originate from East Asians looking back to ancestors across many generations with continuity. The belief manifests itself in many ways, such as a willingness to make long-term investments or plan strategies for distant time horizons. A famous case is Japan's Toyota hybrid car, the Prius. Hybrid technology required huge initial investments when gasoline prices were low. Most other automakers, including some Japanese manufacturers, focused on making profits in the next three to six months and planned just a few years in advance. Toyota looked twenty to thirty years into the future and was willing to forgo years of profits to position itself better in the long run.

East Asians respect a person's social status or hierarchical position, as evidenced in the frequent use of family names or titles. It may have historical origins. Until the early 1800s, many East Asians lived in agricultural societies, often with castelike hierarchies. In a caste society, everyone has a ranked position: semislave, peasant, merchant, warrior, or aristocrat. Engrained status distinctions remained strong even as East Asia underwent industrialization. East Asians are familiar with western ideals of equality, personal freedom, and participatory democracy; however, such ideals have centuries-long roots in the West but are more recent arrivals in East Asia.

Dynamic Youth Culture

Do not think that East Asian culture is only ancient. New elements enter due to innovation or borrowing. East Asia has a vibrant youth-based popular culture. East Asia is also a source of many of the latest technologies and produces music, video games, clothing fashion, and animation. Across Asia young people follow the "Korean wave" of popular music or dramatic films and J-Pop (Japanese music bands).[9] Around the world people sing karaoke or watch anime, both of Japanese origin, and buy other Asian fashion-fad items. Other aspects of Asian culture, such as learning tae kwon do or eating Chinese cuisine with chopsticks, have spread worldwide.

Conclusion

East Asians and Americans both eat pizza, talk on cell phones, drive cars, and wear jeans. Yet they differ in outlooks, daily habits, and thinking patterns arising from rich cultures that go back centuries. East Asian culture is a complex blending of Confucian, Daoist, Buddhist, and local influences. Despite recent East-West exchanges, centuries of separation from the West left enduring Asian cultural differences, and such differences often contribute to misunderstandings.

Worldview difference can be a major source of misunderstanding. Studies by cross-cultural psychologists and cultural anthropologists have found that East Asians and westerners often carry different assumptions and make decisions in different ways due to their cultural worldviews. Westerners tend to see the world as comprised of many separate or fragmented parts, favor taking independent action, and think by using abstract categories or general principles. East Asians tend to adopt more of a parts-of-the-whole, or holistic, perspective. Compared to westerners, they are more willing to cooperate and coordinate their actions with others, think in terms of relationships, and quickly see the interconnections among people or objects.

East Asians and westerners share a great deal, but as the cross-cultural psychologist Richard Nisbett (2003, 87) noted, "There is good reason to believe that Westerners and Asians literally experience the world in very different ways." Learning a very different cultural perspective offers you a window through which to understand East Asia. Yet it requires you to keep an open mind and exert genuine effort. In the next chapter, we examine the family and growing up in East Asia.

FAMILY LIFE IN EAST ASIA

E ach of us lives in a specific family. We also carry an image of the ideal family, rooted in tradition, upheld in teachings, and codified in law. The ideal has symbolic significance and shapes our thinking about families, even when it does not match the daily life of most real families. In this chapter you will learn about ideal and real families in East Asia. As the sociologist Ronald Rindfuss (2004, 136) warned, "Concepts like 'marriage,' 'mother,' and 'son' are not constant across times or societies . . . [and] each of these terms is a culturally and temporally specific set of norms and expectations."

THE IDEAL FAMILY

In traditional Confucian beliefs, the family is the foundation of society. This idea has shaped views on the East Asian ideal family. In the ideal traditional family, children obeyed parental wishes, parents arranged spouse selection, and a successful marriage joined two family lineages rather than fulfilling the romantic desires of two individuals. A new bride left her birth family and moved into her husband's multigenerational family residence to become part of his family. As a female outsider, she was the lowest-ranked family member, almost a servant. She was obligated to obey her mother-in-law's dictates, adopt her husband's family customs, and worship their ancestors. She remained part of his family, even after his death.[1]

The ideal family emphasized continuing an ancestral bloodline. In practice this put intense pressure on a married woman to produce a son who could be the next family heir. In the past failure to bear a son might result in divorce, with the disgraced bride returned to her birth family. For many in East Asia, bloodline defines family, even today. Adoption was acceptable in Japan, but rarely elsewhere. Japanese couples without a surviving child could adopt sons, and couples with only a surviving daughter could adopt a son-in-law. In the traditional ideal family, sons were the focus, because daughters had little value. A daughter was not a permanent family member but left to join another family on marriage, costing her family a dowry in the process.[2]

Social relations within the traditional ideal family followed a strict gender and age order. The divorced or unmarried woman was almost a nonperson with few opportunities. A married woman was to obey and serve her husband, other males, and elders; should not work outside the home; and could not initiate a divorce. As an "inside person," she was rarely seen outside the home. There she was the first up in the morning and last to bed at night. Ideally, she was a self-sacrificing daughter-in-law, an obedient and dutiful wife, and a wise and caring mother. Husbands held family authority and ruled over relationships outside the home that affected the family.

The central relationship was parent and child, especially father and son, not husband and wife. Obedience, not equal democratic decision making, was a virtue. A husband might have sexual relations with other women, and the practice of having a live-in concubine continued in parts of East Asia into the early twentieth century. Yet a wife was to marry as a virgin and always remain modest. Public expressions of spousal affection or vows of romantic love were, and to an extent still are, considered in poor taste.[3]

You may have heard of the nuclear or conjugal family. It consists of a married couple and their children. The extended family includes relatives such as grandparents, uncles and aunts, cousins, and so forth. Family anthropologists and sociologists identify two types of extended families— *stem* and *joint* families. Both are common in preindustrial societies. They classify the traditional East Asian family system as a *stem family*. It has a couple and their eldest son, plus that son's spouse and children, coresiding in one household until the parents' deaths. A *joint family* has a couple, possibility their siblings with spouses and children, and/or the main couple's adult children with their spouses and children. Together, they form one household unit, reside together or nearby, interact daily, and cooperate by sharing work and resources within the large household. Until recently, the stem family was widespread in East Asia, although the joint family was common in parts of rural China. Across East Asia the nuclear family form is increasingly common.[4]

The ideal traditional family has three other features: primogeniture and patrilineal and patrilocal relationships. *Primogeniture* refers to ranking male children by age and giving most or all of the family inheritance to the eldest son. *Patrilineal* means tracing ancestry through the male line. *Patrilocal* means that a newly married couple resides with the husband's parents or moves to his village. A stem family with primogeniture grows like a tree: the eldest son continues the tree trunk following his father and male ancestors. He inherits family leadership responsibility and all or most of the family property and becomes the new family patriarch. Younger sons are branches that extend outward from the family tree's trunk; although they move into separate residences after marriage, they remain connected to the family.

REAL FAMILIES

Life in many, or even most, past and contemporary East Asian families has not matched the ideal. Many factors shape life in real families: local customs and morals, habitual practices, and social pressures from relatives and neighbors. All may cause the family unit to diverge from the ideal. For example, in some East Asian villages the newly married couple does not join the husband's family. During the Qin dynasty and the Chinese Republic era, *fenjia*, dividing property equally among brothers, was common. Politics may seem remote from families, but it, too, can influence real family life. When the Chinese Communist Party changed marriage law in 1950, it overturned centuries of custom and practice by abolishing arranged marriages, ending child brides and concubines, granting women the right to divorce, and declaring husband and wife to be legal equals. The government also broke up family farms with collectivization, ended inheritance, and outlawed many traditional practices. Catastrophes, such as foreign invasion, war, or famine, periodically disrupt family life. Japan's invasion of China, the Chinese Cultural Revolution, Korea's war and division, and Japan's defeat and occupation created millions of orphans, widows, and dislocated people. Separated from past family attachments, traditional patterns loosened as people rebuilt their lives and forged new family relationships.

Economic circumstances also shaped family life. East Asian ideal family patterns were largely rooted in the landowners of an agricultural economy, and few poor peasant or tenant farm families could adhere to the ideal. As East Asia industrialized, millions of sons or daughters left home to attend school or work in distant locations, and this realigned family relations. In the late nineteenth and early twentieth centuries, schooling, mass media, and foreign sources spread new ideas about the family. In the late twentieth century, younger generations questioned arranged marriages, some husbands began to care for infant children, married women sought full-time paid work outside the home, and increasing numbers of elderly parents wanted to live independent of their son's family.

In the ideal traditional family, wives wanted many children. Today's East Asian women are having few children. Family size in East Asia has declined, as it has in all industrialized societies. Now fewer children are born than what is required to maintain population size (see table 3.2). China's "one-child policy," adopted in the late 1970s, is well known. It has been less strictly enforced in rural areas and has exemptions, such as for ethnic minority families. In fact Chinese women are having more children on average (1.55) than occurs in countries lacking an official policy to limit births (e.g., Taiwan, Japan, or South Korea with birth rates of 1.16, 1.39, and 1.23 respectfully).

While many features of the ideal traditional family have faded away, other features persist. We see traditional customs in marriage ceremonies, in the practice of referring to one another by family position (e.g., elder sister, uncle) rather than personal name, in the great respect shown to ancestors, and in the high value placed on filial piety.

Filial Piety and Ancestors

Filial piety has shaped social life across East Asia for centuries and was at the core of the ideal traditional family. A fundamental tenet of filial piety is that children have a moral duty to obey, respect, and care for parents and elders. The duty extends to respecting family ancestors and overrides personal ambitions, impulses, and desires. The value of filial piety permeates East Asian ethical teachings and popular beliefs. It is repeated in song lyrics, poetry and folktales, movie and novel plots, and legal rulings.

Beyond being a cultural value that shapes self-image, ideals, and priorities, filial piety also has practical consequences. It dictates proper living arrangements, sets rules for owning and transferring property, and outlines who owes whom financial support. As a kind of intergenerational social contract, filial piety says that parents sacrifice for years to raise and care for children and then transfer their wealth to them. In return children owe parents a huge moral and material debt.[5]

Filial piety gave rise to a family-based system of old-age assistance, health care, and social welfare before today's pensions or public aid programs. For example, you will see relatively few old-age homes in East

42

Asia in part because of a widespread belief that every upright, decent adult child should care for or live with his or her elderly parents (see table 3.1).

Table 3.1. Attitudes About and Rates of Coresidence in East Asia

Attitude or Behavior	China	Japan	S. Korea	Taiwan
Percentage that say coresidence with elderly parents is desirable	56	66	59	73
Percentage that say eldest son is responsible for parents	14	14	44	16
Percentage of adult couples that live with elderly parents (when husband's or wife's parents are alive)	24	27	10	39

Source: Yasuda et al. 2011.

COURTSHIP, SPOUSE SELECTION, AND MARRIAGE

Finding a marriage partner occupies the attention of most young adults, but who makes an acceptable or desirable partner varies by society and era. The community and family may impose limits based on religion, educational level, social class, age, health status, ethnicity, and so forth. Arranged marriages were common before the twentieth century in many world regions, but the practice continued among East Asia's upper and middle classes well into the twentieth century.

Figure 3.1. Wedding in a Japanese park (Author photo).

In recent decades East Asians increasingly have selected their own spouses, or have a "love marriage." Arranged marriage officially ended in China in 1950 with a new marriage law, although some informal arranging continues in rural areas. In Taiwan about two-thirds of all marriages were arranged in the 1930s, but by the 1960s only about 10 percent were arranged. Almost half of South Korean couples had an arranged marriage in the 1980s, but only one-fourth did by the mid-1990s. As late as the 1990s, 20 to 30 percent of all Japanese had arranged marriages, but the practice continues to decline.[6]

The events leading up to selecting a marriage partner are more complicated than a simple division between an arranged and a love marriage. Oftentimes even the couple cannot say whether they have an arranged or love marriage. Nearly all twenty-first-century East Asian couples chose their own marriage partner, but most also retain a strong belief that parents should be involved and give consent. Many rely on coworkers, family members, or professional matchmakers to help locate a potential partner and arrange initial introductions. After they meet it is up to the couple to develop mutual affection and have the final say. Unlike in most western countries, in East Asia serious male-female dating rarely begins prior to the college years, and mixed-sex group dates are more common than couple dates.[7] For many South Koreans a woman's education is a prestige symbol and more useful for the roles of wife and mother than as preparation for a professional career.[8]

Declining parental influence over spouse selection coincided with a shift in the purpose of marriage. Financial stability, status improvement, and family alliance building remain important factors, but romance, shared interests, and companionship are superseding them. Nonetheless, young East Asians emphasize family approval and practical concerns, and they tend to view marriage less positively than westerners, who prioritize romantic love and personal happiness in a marriage.

Many young people engage in sexual relations before marriage. Forbidden in the ideal family, many in the landowning classes obeyed the prohibition, except for men who visited "pleasure quarters." Widespread premarital sex among peasants in rural villages declined as formal schooling and modern communication spread in the twentieth century. In recent decades, sexual relations among unmarried adults have gained wide social acceptance across East Asia. Although premarital sexual behavior has spread, living together before marriage has not. In the United States, about 10 percent of adults cohabit and one-half of married couples previously cohabitated. Rates in the United States are in the middle of international comparisons, with cohabitation more common in Sweden or France, and less so in Italy. In East Asia only 2 to 3 percent of young adults are cohabiting, and fewer than 10 percent of married couples ever cohabited. However, Japan has seen a recent sharp rise in cohabitation rates.[9]

Americans tend to marry younger than adults in other western countries do. In recent decades the worldwide trend has been for age at marriage to increase. Age at marriage has also risen in Japan, Taiwan, and South Korea (see table 3.2), as has the mother's age at the birth of her first child. For example, in Japan and South Korea about 80 percent of women were married by age twenty-five in the 1950s. Today only 20 percent are married by that age. China is more complex due to its internal diversity and pressures to marry late during the Maoist era. As pressures relaxed with post-Maoist reforms and liberalization in the 1980s and 1990s, age at marriage has declined in China.

Divorce has been rare in East Asia. Traditionally, only a husband could initiate it. By the twenty-first century, divorce rates were rising as traditional restrictions relaxed and individual legal rights expanded.[10] Currently, East Asian divorce rates are only slightly lower than those of other industrialized nations and the stigma of divorce is fading.

FAMILY REGISTRATION

Most governments maintain a registration system with information on all citizens (e.g., residence, births, deaths, marriages). For centuries East Asian governments registered family units, not individuals. Household registers in China and Japan date back to seventh century or earlier. Early Meiji era Japan revised its registration system into the *koskei* (family registry) that remains today. Korea adopted the *hoju*, a family registration system similar to the koseki, in 1898. The CCP kept the imperial *hukou* registration system when it took power in 1949 but significantly revised it. Taiwan adopted a *koseki* system when it was a Japanese colony and continues to use a modified version of it.[11]

Japan's *koseki* began as a way to keep track of males for military conscription but grew into a comprehensive family registration system, recording all births, adoptions, deaths, marriages, and divorces. Meiji era leaders promoted a "family nation" ideal, with the emperor as a father figure for all Japanese. The 1898 Meiji Civil Code included an ideal Japanese family, the *ie*, modeled on Confucian principles and the samurai family. The *ie* household spans many generations to include grandparents,

45

Table 3.2. Comparison of Marriage, Divorce, and Birth Statistics

Country	Women Age 16–64 Employed (%)	Divorce Rate per 1,000 Population	Male Average Age at First Marriage	Female Average Age at First Marriage	Average Births per Woman
China	76	1.6	33.8	29.1	1.55
Taiwan	49	2.75	31.8	29.4	1.16
South Korea	54	2.4	31.6	28.7	1.23
Japan	61	1.8	29.4	27.6	1.39
United States	70	3.4	28.4	26.5	2.06
Canada	73	2.2	30.6	28.5	1.58

Note: Most data are for 2008–12, but they vary by country and item. All websites were accessed on January 26, 2014.

Sources: Female labor force participation: World Bank, World Development Indicators database, except Taiwan, which is http://eng.stat.gov.tw/public/data/dgbas03/bs2/gender/Images%20of%20Women.pdf. Age at first marriage: United Nations, Department of Economic and Social Affairs, Population Division. World Marriage Data 2008 (POP/DB/Marr/Rev2008), except Taiwan, which is http://focustaiwan.tw/search/201305250018.aspx?q=Marriage. Divorce rate: http://unstats.un.org/unsd/demographic/products/dyb/dyb2008/Table25.pdf, except the United States, which is http://www.cdc.gov/nchs/nvss/marriage_divorce_tables.htm, and Taiwan, which is http://www.taiwan.gov.tw/ct.asp?xItem=105399&ctNode=1918&mp=999. Average number of births per woman: CIA Factbook (2012 estimates).

parents with their eldest son, his wife, and their children. The male head of the family has absolute authority within the family, including decisions over property and inheritance, where family members live, and approval of marriages and divorces. Japan's family law endorsed the *ie* until 1947 when the American Occupation forced its abolition, yet many families retain some of its features as a cultural tradition.[12]

After the U.S. Occupation, Japan's government continued the *koseki*. While the *koseki* is currently kept in a local government office, until the 1970s employers, prospective marriage partners, and almost anyone could view a person's family history in it (including illegitimate children, adoptions, divorces, etc.), sometimes resulting in discrimination. Today only people in the *koskei* and those directly involved in a legal action (e.g., criminal violation, debt collection, or inheritance claim) can view it.

China used the *hukou* family register of births, deaths, marriages, divorces, and residence for centuries. In the 1950s China's Communist government revised it into a residence permit system modeled on the Soviet Union's internal passport system, which the government used to control population movement between rural and urban areas. Until the economic reforms that occurred after 1978, a Chinese citizen could not move to a different town or take a job elsewhere without official permission. All adult residents had a government-determined job, which provided access to housing, health care, schooling, food, and local services. After the market economy reforms, the *hukou* system weakened. Today about two hundred million people from rural areas live outside their official *hukou* areas, having migrated to fast-growing cities for work in China's booming economy. However, outside their *hukou* residences they are like illegal immigrants. Local governments may deny them schooling and public services. The national government also uses the *hukou* to gather demographic data for planning and to monitor political dissidents.

Japanese colonial authorities, following Confucian ideals, set up Korea's *hoju* family register. It listed family members in order under the male family head, then sons and grandsons, then the females, including the male head's mother, wife, daughters, granddaughters, and daughters-in-law. Korea's government abolished the *hoju* and replaced it with an individual registration system after revisions were made to family law in 2005 to improve gender equality.[13]

CHILD REARING AND MULTIGENERATIONAL HOUSEHOLDS

Child care responsibilities vary by gender in most countries, but this is especially true in East Asia. Fathers in both the ideal and most real families do little, and mothers alone are responsible for nurturing and raising the children. Despite her subservient role, a mother gains moral authority and influence through child rearing. After all, she gives birth to the next family heir, supervises and maintains harmony within a household, raises and instructs the family's next generation, and secures marriage matches for her children. Traditionally, the husband was responsible for a family's economic situation and outside-world relations, while the wife upheld the family's face, facilitated children's success, and ensured family continuation into the next generation.

The emphasis on a wife's childbearing and rearing roles helps to explain why few East Asian mothers with young children work outside the home. Only in the past fifteen years, as women have had fewer children

Figure 3.2. Elderly Japanese couple not living
with their children (Author photo).

and acquired more education, have very large numbers worked outside the home. In Japan, Taiwan, and South Korea, about 20 percent of women with young children (under six) are working outside the home with variations by country. By contrast, in the United States nearly 60 percent of mothers with young children work outside the home. China is an exception. Since 1950, China's government has promoted full-time work for all men and women, and it has had one of the world's highest female labor force participation rates. In a trend that differs from elsewhere, Chinese rates of married women working outside the home have declined somewhat since the 1980s, after the post-Maoist market reforms.[14]

The tradition of a couple living with or close to grandparents facilitated the practice of grandparent child care, and grandparents are often integral to child rearing. Until very recently, Korea, Japan, and Taiwan had few professional child care facilities. During China's Maoist years, state enterprises or communes provided child care. However, since the 1980s economic reforms, few families, except the wealthy, can afford professional child care. Instead most Chinese families rely on grandparents, relatives, neighbors, or informal private babysitters.[15]

"Living with grandma," or the three-generation household, is rare in the United States (under 15 percent of families). It was once common practice in East Asia, although it has been on the decline. The percentage of Japanese elderly persons who live with an adult child dropped from 80 percent in 1950 to 50 percent in the 1990s, then to about 25 percent. In South Korea the decline was from 78 percent in 1984 to 47 percent in 1994. In Taiwan it dropped from 82 percent in 1973 to 70 percent in 1986. A social belief that living with elderly parents is desirable remains strong even if it is no longer the majority practice (see table 3.1). Fewer families are "living with grandma," but this traditional practice provides child care that has allowed more mothers to work outside the home.[16]

In the past two decades, the elderly are increasingly living as separate couples or alone. The "networked family" is replacing the multigenerational household. In it three generations live close by and frequently interact, exchanging services and providing support. Changing attitudes and practical factors, such as the availability of pensions, rising living standards, and life in congested large cities with tight housing space, explain the decline of multigenerational families.[17]

Confucian beliefs that endow formal schooling with great respect, a fervent desire to advance a family's social and economic position, and seeing sons as family heirs have combined to encourage making large family investments in a son's schooling (schooling is discussed in chapter 4). Far more than most western families, East Asian families invest a great deal in their children's education and create pressure for success in school. Many middle-income families in Japan, South Korea, and Taiwan take out second mortgages or a parent takes on a job solely to pay for a child's school expenses. Japan has a term *kyōiku mama*, "education mother." It describes mothers who devote their lives to ensuring their child's educational success. They buy expensive school supplies, attend numerous parent-teacher meetings, help with homework, and take on jobs to pay for high-cost tutors or cram schools. Parental focus on education often starts before kindergarten and continues in high school and college. South Koreans may be even more focused on education than the Japanese are, and intense attention to a child's school success is true of many families across East Asian cultures.[18]

HOUSEWORK

When the children are young, few East Asian mothers, except the Chinese, work outside the home. Nonetheless, most adult women work do outside

Figure 3.3. A young, egalitarian Japanese couple (Author photo).

the home full or part time (nearly 75 percent of Chinese, 70 percent of Japanese, and 60 percent of South Koreans and Taiwanese). In Japan, South Korea, and Taiwan we see an "M curve," which describes changing rates for women working across the life cycle. Shaped like the letter *M*, it shows that few women are working immediately after high school because they are attending a technical or junior college or university. By their early to midtwenties, most join the work force, and rates of working peak. Rates then sharply plummet for women in their late twenties to midthirties with marriage and the birth of a child. Working rates slowly rise as children get older and enter school. They hit a second peak for women in their early forties to midfifties as mothers return to the work force to supplement family income and cover educational expenses. Rates decline as women reach their late fifties to early sixties and approach retirement age. In South Korea and Japan, most mothers work part time, while in Taiwan and China full-time work for all women is more common.[19]

In most societies wives do the bulk of housework (cooking, cleaning, etc.). In East Asia husbands do even less housework than their western counterparts. Ten percent of American husbands never help with the housework, but 43 percent of Japanese and 32 percent of South Korean husbands never help. Fifty- to sixty-hour workweeks, long commutes, and pressure to socialize with coworkers after work combine so that men may be away from home seventy-two hours or more a week. This, plus entrenched attitudes and workplace gender inequality, explains why few men help. A small percentage of young Japanese husbands have embraced egalitarian family relations. Compared to South Korea or Japan, husbands in Taiwan and China tend to do more housework.[20]

Gender equality in doing housework in China was encouraged by high rates of women working outside the home and official policies that promoted gender equality. However, since the economic reforms of the 1980s, gender inequality has returned to China. The CCP emphasis on gender equality, public policies, and equal gender employment in the public sector has given way to less government interference and less regulated private sector practices (discussed in more detail in the chapter 5).

CONCLUSION

East Asians appear to be leaving traditional ideals behind and converging on western family patterns as globalization and modernization weaken lingering Confucian influences on the family. Today East Asians and westerners differ little with respect to family size, abortion rates, average births per woman, a trend toward later marriage, and both spouses working outside the home. In the last two decades, East Asia has experienced dramatic fertility declines and an aging population.

Yet convergence is only part of the picture. Multiple family forms coexist in both eastern and western societies, and East Asia has national, regional, and rural-urban variations. Despite some convergence, real differences remain. Filial piety is fading slowly. Compared to most westerners, young East Asian adults tend to start dating later, rely more on others to help with matchmaking, and be more concerned about parental approval of a potential spouse. They are also less likely to cohabit, marry early, or give birth before marriage. In general East Asians view marriage and family in practical terms with a long-term orientation more than is common among westerners. Parents invest heavily in a child's schooling and then tend to live with or close to married sons, daughters-in-law, and grandchildren. The adult children often provide their elderly parents with ongoing physical, emotional, and financial support. Instead of a global convergence toward a uniform family form or a unique East Asian family type, we see in East Asian families a mixture of persistent features along with the gradual influence of broad international trends.

4

School and the Transition to Work

School is the center of our lives and molds awareness during the formative years of development. A nation's culture, history, and politics shape its schooling. By young adulthood, the workplace replaces school and provides a social position and identity, an income source, and a network of coworkers. Work settings vary widely. People spend years standing in muddy fields, sitting behind a desk in front of a computer screen, toiling on an assembly line, listening to and examining patients, standing at a cash register, and so forth. Societal context structures a nation's economy, and world events affect work life. After working for thirty to forty years, people move into retirement. In this chapter we examine schooling and work.

Schooling Differences

Across East Asia schools look familiar on the surface, except for the many schoolchildren in uniforms. Children proceed through a sequence of grades (e.g., elementary, junior high, and high school), sit at a desk in a classroom, carry notebooks and textbooks, and have lessons from professionally trained teachers in schools with gyms, auditoriums, libraries, and playgrounds. The curriculum includes reading, writing, arithmetic, history, science, art and music, and physical education.

Despite surface similarities, a closer comparison reveals a more complex picture. East Asian students regularly score at the top of international math, science, and reading skills tests, virtually all who begin high school graduate on time, and several East Asian nations lead the world in the percentage of high school graduates who continue on to a university education. By contrast American students score near the middle in international tests, one in four students who starts high school fails to finish, and the United States has fallen to twelfth of thirty-six among

Figure 4.1. Japanese students in school uniform (Author photo).

developed nations in percentage of high school graduates continuing on to university.[1]

National values and beliefs shape how schools prepare children to become adult members of society. As you learned from past chapters, the Confucian tradition emphasizes self-improvement, instills respect for learning and teachers, and elevates filial piety, both as an obligation of children to care for parents and as a sign of moral worth. East Asian children learn that if they succeed in school they will develop into a worthy person, honor their parents, and uphold the reputations of family and ancestors. East Asian schools reinforce related values: deference to hierarchy, self-discipline, and a sense of collective responsibility.

Cultural priorities permeate school life. What one culture criticizes or treats as undesirable might be acceptable or even valued by another. For example, a study of preschools in three cultures found that American preschool teachers sought to teach children to make individual choices, and they intervened to stop fights among children, feeling that fighting is morally wrong and fearing emotional or physical harm to a child. Japanese teachers made building empathy for others a top priority and rarely stopped fights so they could encourage children to develop their own conflict resolution skills. Chinese preschool teachers had children tell stories before a class and then encouraged other students to criticize the storyteller. Instead of exhibiting concern about the storytelling child's self-esteem, they sought to teach the children how to give and take direct criticism.[2]

Parental expectations and beliefs about academic success vary by culture. A study comparing Japanese, Chinese, and American elementary school children found dramatic differences in parental involvement, attitudes, and expectations.

> Whereas children's academic achievement did not appear to be a central concern of American mothers, Chinese and Japanese mothers viewed this as their child's most important pursuit. . . . American mothers appeared to be less interested in their child's academic achievement than in the child's general cognitive development; they attempted to provide experiences that fostered cognitive growth rather than academic excellence. Chinese and Japanese mothers held higher standards for their children's achievement than American mothers and gave more realistic evaluations of their child's academic, cognitive, and personality characteristics. American mothers overestimated their child's abilities and expressed greater satisfaction with their child's accomplishments than the Chinese and Japanese mothers. In describing bases of children's academic achievement, Chinese and Japanese mothers stressed the importance of hard work to a greater degree than American mothers, and American mothers gave greater emphasis to innate ability. (Stevenson and Lee 1990, v–vi)

Figure 4.2. A Korean high school classroom (Author photo).

Figure 4.3. A Japanese kindergarten class (Author photo).

East Asian mothers actively assisted in a child's learning and emphasized internal motivation, so that children valued learning for its own sake. By contrast American mothers gave teachers the primary responsibility for learning and emphasized external rewards (e.g., good grades or access to a high-paying job). While East Asian mothers pushed their children to succeed, American mothers expressed a fear that pressure to excel in school could harm a child psychologically.

Beyond cultural differences, East Asia and the United States have many institutional differences, such as the amount of time devoted to learning. The U.S. school year varies by state, but K–12 schooling across East Asia is a month to six weeks longer (See table 4.1). Japan phased out Saturday classes, 1990s to 2002. However, after public debate Saturday classes returned to many schools in 2007 based on an option available to local school administrations. A typical Japanese youth will have spent over two additional years doing schoolwork by high school graduation than an American does. Japan is not unique. The Taiwanese education professors Chou and Ho (2007, 365) reported, "Unlike many Western counterparts who attend school from 9 a.m. to 3 p.m., Taiwanese secondary students have a much longer school day from 7:30 a.m. to 5:30 p.m." The U.S. school year still follows a nineteenth-century agrarian calendar, starting in September and ending in early June with a three-month summer vacation. East Asian school years start in other seasons and have shorter vacations.

Table 4.1. Comparison of Ten- and Eleven-Year-Old Children in 2006

Country	School Year (Days)	School Year Start	Years of Compulsary Schooling	Percentage Finishing High School	Average K–12 Class Size
South Korea	220–222	March	9	97%	49
Taiwan	222	September	9	96%	44
China	200–251	September	9	Est. 40–50%	39
Japan	220–243	April	9	97%	40–50
USA	178–180	August/ September	12	Est. 70–80%	23

Sources: http://www.boojle.com/forums/archive/index.php/t-5604.html (accessed on August 15, 2012); http://nces.ed.gov/pubs/eiip/eiipid24.asp http://nces.ed.gov/pubs98/yi/ yi38.pdf (accessed on January 26, 2014); http://Nationmaster.com Chuing and Ho 2007; Dillon 2008; Khadaroo 2010 (accessed on January 26, 2014).

Location of school control is another institutional difference. Although there is variation by state, the U.S. public school system is among the world's most decentralized; locally elected school boards and state-level Departments of Education make most decisions. By contrast national Ministries of Education across East Asia have a major say over issues such as teacher training, curriculum, school policies and standards, and textbooks. Over the past decade, other groups are beginning to have some say, and centralized control has slowly weakened.

A third difference is class size. North Americans and Europeans demand small classes to allow individualized attention from teachers, and the average U.S. K–12 class has twenty-three students. Class sizes in East Asia are almost twice as large. Even preschools might have thirty-five children in a class with two teachers. Differences in class size reflect dissimilar values and priorities. Americans value individualism and emphasize cognitive skill acquisition. East Asians want to build collective identity and teach the whole child. Most East Asian schools also have an explicit moral education curriculum, in contrast to a prohibition on or aversion to teaching morality in U.S. public schools.[3]

Another difference is the teaching profession. Despite significant state and regional variation, in general U.S. teachers are not highly esteemed or rewarded. East Asian teachers receive high status, and teaching is a well-paid profession. Comparing teacher pay internationally is complicated, but after adjustments East Asians pay K–12 teachers very well. In 2009 a Japanese K–12 public school teacher earned about ten thousand dollars and a Korean teacher about thirty-five thousand dollars more per year than teachers in the United States, United Kingdom, and Australia. In Taiwan competition to enter the teaching field is intense, and the field attracts high-achieving college-bound students. All teacher-training colleges are public and offer tuition waivers, as well as free housing, supplies, and books, in exchange for five years of service at a government-determined location. Teacher salaries are higher than those of civil servants with similar qualifications, and teachers also receive an income tax exemption.[4] The Chinese situation is an exception, and teacher pay, especially in rural areas, is lower than elsewhere in East Asia.

Another institutional difference is when and how youths make their way into divergent adult livelihoods. The United States has a highly varied, flexible school-to-work transition system. Schooling is compulsory to age sixteen to eighteen (it varies by state) and is free to grade twelve. Those who drop out before high school graduation are "on their own" in the working world. For high school graduates, paths diverge into the working world, a vocational-technical school, or a university. The quality and status distinctions among high schools and universities are large but vague and not officially recognized. University entrance depends on a mix of high school grades, test scores, and parental resources. Students have options for admittance at various ages, financial aid is available, and a student can transfer among universities. Finding postschool employment is haphazard and depends on a mix of placement services, individual initiative, and personal connections.

East Asia's school-to-work linkages are well integrated. Compulsory education ends at age fourteen or fifteen (grade nine or ten), and then distinct pathways open up. Most youths voluntarily continue on to high school. High schools have a vocational or academic orientation, and entrance is by examination. Vocational high schools provide practical career preparation and then connect students to employers. Academic high schools concentrate on university preparation and are ranked based how many graduates can enter top universities. The ranks and prestige of universities are serious, well known, and consequential. University entrance is by examination score and limited to shortly after high school. The top universities do not cost more than low-ranked ones. Scholarships are rare, as is the ability to transfer among universities. Leading public and private sector employers that offer the best pay and job security recruit exclusively at top-ranked universities and hire new graduates not

Figure 4.4. A junior high math class in Taiwan. Source:
http://commons.wikimedia.org/wiki/File:Math_class_in_
Chu_Jen_Junior_High_School_2007-08-23.jpg.

midcareer people. Few paths to the best careers and financial rewards are available to those who do not attend a highly ranked university. Students with low high school entrance test scores are directed to vocational or low-prestige high schools. They will enter lower paying occupations or less prestigious universities or technical colleges that lead to less secure or rewarded careers. The East Asian school-to-work system is less open and chaotic than that of the United States, but it is not rigid. Rather, it has a few critical juncture points and rarely offers second chances for teens who are late bloomers, lack discipline and seriousness, or make poor personal life decisions.[5]

THE EXAMINATION SYSTEM

East Asia's "high-stakes" entrance examinations attract much attention. Most teens devote tremendous time and energy to passing a few critical examinations that can open up or close off divergent futures. Examinations are pervasive. Andrew Kipnis, an anthropologist who has studied China's school system, noted (2011, 121), "Not only are there exams for university entrance, senior middle school entrance, graduate school entrance, and almost every variety of diploma available, but outside of education the exams are also widespread in the recruitment of employees in both the public and private sector." Examinations are a motivator and create a powerful incentive to study diligently because their consequences are decisive. Despite its imperfections, East Asians embrace the examination system over alternative ways to allocate people to different life paths.

East Asia's examination system began in Han China (201 BCE–8 CE). A male had to pass an examination, *keju*, to acquire a secure position in the emperor's service. Examinations advanced people by merit and weakened regional divisions and local aristocratic power in imperial China. Korea and Japan adopted versions of China's examinations, although their use varied by era and country. For example, Japanese nobles could avoid taking the examination and still assume a high government post. In the nineteenth century, European and North American nations adopted versions of the examination system as they created civil service systems. In the Meiji era, Japan revamped the examination system, expanded it in schooling, and exported it to the colonies of Taiwan and Korea. The system fell into disfavor with the rise of Communist Party rule in China in 1949 and disappeared in 1966 with the Cultural Revolution. Until the mid-1970s, China instead selected leaders based on family class position (e.g., landlord, peasant, or worker), patriotism, and commitment to Maoist ideology. Since the late 1970s, China has returned to reliance on the examination system.[6]

The college entrance examination is an all-day test administered nationwide once a year on a range of subjects (e.g., language, history, mathematics, and science). Examination results, not high school grades, extracurricular activities, parental wealth, or letters of recommendation, determine who enters a top university. Some low-scoring students delay college, study for a year, then retake the examination in an attempt to improve their scores. They are called *rōnin* in Japanese, meaning "lordless samurai." In recent years some low-quality private universities have begun to exempt students from taking the examination in order to expand tuition-paying enrollment.

Media pundits and educational experts in the West and Asia have criticized the examination system for its emphasis on passing a test over true learning and for generating great emotional distress. An "all or nothing" examination encourages students to memorize rather than develop critical thinking, acquire broad-based knowledge, expand creativity, or master practical problem-solving skills. It also creates intense pressure, which the media sensationalizes when a youth commits suicide after failing a test.

Despite the publicity, little solid evidence supports claims of mindless rote learning, high teen suicide rates, and emotional-psychological damage. Classroom observers found some rote learning in some grade levels, yet teen suicide rates differ little from those found elsewhere, and East Asian schoolchildren report feeling less stress and enjoying school more than American children do. Individual students may experience intense anxiety shortly before an examination, but many media reports are exaggerated.[7]

The examination system persists for several reasons: it keeps students occupied and "away from trouble," it provides a clear path upward, and it has legitimacy. People accept it as a fair, objective way to select future leaders. When it works as intended, advancing to a high position requires an individual's diligence, persistence, and achievement in a competitive, merit-based process that is open to all comers. Advancement is not due to a person having more financial resources, favoritism, or family connections.

The examination system has spawned a huge industry in private after-school enrichment or "cram" schools and private tutors. Junior high and high school students may attend a *juku* (Japan), *buxiban* (Taiwan), or *hakwon* (Korea) one or more days a week. Participation varies by grade level, urban-rural area, and country, but an estimated 75 percent of East Asian students attend a supplemental school at some point (versus less than 10 percent of American children). Some review and reinforce regular classroom learning, others offer enrichment activities, and still others drill students in test preparation.[8]

We need to situate the cram school industry in the context of the examination system and cultural respect for formal schooling. Compared to East Asian children, most American children do less homework, watch more TV, and believe they have already learned enough in school. A typical American fourteen to sixteen years old is preoccupied with dating and romance five years sooner than most East Asian adolescents are. If an American child participates in an after-school activity, it is likely to be sports related rather than academically oriented. It almost never involves studying a foreign language. Children everywhere absorb broad cultural values and embrace them as personal beliefs and attitudes. Take the desire to make money: American children more than those in East Asia believe "I will be happy if I am rich."[9]

Not surprisingly, more high-income than low-income families purchase after-school education. Well-educated, high-income East Asian families rely on supplemental schools to improve their children's chances to attain financial and career success. Well-educated, high-income

American families buy houses in areas with better school districts or pay private school tuition for the same reason. The supplemental school industry is simply a response to East Asian families that are trying to transmit family class position to the next generation in a context that has few alternatives to the examination system.[10] East Asian families spend two to three times more on schooling, as a percentage of household income, than American families do. The prime reasons are paying for supplemental schools, greater reliance on private high schools and universities, and a near absence of financial aid for schooling.[11]

COUNTRY DIFFERENCES

Thus far we have focused on East Asia as a whole, but schools vary by country and change over time. As the first Asian country to industrialize and modernize, others looked to Japan's schools. Officials of the U.S. Occupation forces tried to remold Japan's school system to make it more like that of the United States, but they had limited to moderate success. Under U.S. pressure, strict political indoctrination ceased, high schools became gender integrated and comprehensive, and centralized control weakened. We have seen three trends in Japan since the beginning of this century: less gender separation in higher education, reduced intensity and greater flexibility in K–12 schooling, and a demographic implosion in higher education.

Until the 1990s Japanese higher education had a sharp gender division. Men attended four-year universities or two-year technical schools, while women entered 90 percent female two-year junior colleges that taught home management, traditional arts, foreign languages, and child care. In 1995, 41 percent of all males attended a four-year university (vs. 23 percent of females) and 2 percent a junior college (vs. 25 percent of females). By 2009 females nearly matched males' four-year university attendance, and the percentage going to a junior college declined by half. Many junior colleges closed or converted to four-year private universities.[12]

Concerns have grown over media reports about school bullying, dropouts, disruptive classrooms, and refusals to attend school. Japan's K–12 schooling faces contradictory reform pressures.[13] Some reformers want a lighter, less-intense curriculum, more local flexibility, encouragement of student creativity, and no Saturday classes. Others want a return to traditional rigor. They advocate nationalistic political lessons and punishing teachers who fail to demonstrate sufficient patriotism. Many Japanese youths have become discouraged by the educational system and their long-term prospects.[14]

Japan's low birth rate and aging population created a situation in which the number of university openings now exceeds the number of high school graduates. Competition for university entry is disappearing, and the lowest quality private universities face closure. At the same time, the national government has increased university autonomy, encouraged university competition, and reduced funding while pushing for closer university–private sector ties. Strong competition to enter elite universities remains, but overall educational competition has sharply declined.

Japan permitted only limited schooling beyond the primary level in both South Korea and Taiwan during the decades of colonial rule. As a result half the population was illiterate when Japanese rule ended. Both countries made expanding primary schooling a top priority in the 1950s. By the 1960s primary schooling had become free and universal in both South Korea and Taiwan. Entrance into middle school was by competitive exam. After this ended in the 1960s, competition shifted to high school entrance. In the 1960s through the 1980s, both countries rapidly expanded their vocational high schools to support a program of industrial development. Between the 1970s and 1990s, high school education became universal. Parents sought an academic high school education that could lead to postsecondary education for their children. As a result academic high school enrollment now greatly outpaces that of vocational high schools.[15]

During the 1980s, both Korea and Taiwan moved from military-backed, nondemocratic rule to open democracies. South Korean university students played a major role in the transition, often engaging in violent political demonstrations, but this was not the case in Taiwan.[16] Competition for college entrance is high in both countries. Currently over 80 percent of South Korean high school graduates enter postsecondary education, the world's highest rate. The government has unsuccessfully attempted to limit supplemental schooling and the expansion of higher education. Rapid growth of higher education has produced many low-quality universities, although competition to enter top-tier universities remains intense. South Korea, like other nations, is facing a major demographic decline. It is estimated that the number of college students will drop from 3.2 million in 2000 to 1.5 million by 2030. As in Japan, this will increase competition for students, create lower admission standards, and cause weaker universities to close.

In Taiwan the number of postsecondary institutions grew by one-third between 1987 and 2004, mostly due to the growth of private institutions. They now account for about 70 percent of total enrollment. Nonetheless, national universities remain respected and prestigious. Higher education enrollment grew from 37.5 percent of the eighteen-to twenty-year-old age group in 1991 to 84 percent by 2010 according to the *Statistical Yearbook of the Republic of China*. As with other nations, Taiwan will face a projected demographic decline in its college-age population in the next decade.

China's situation differs significantly from those of other East Asian countries.[17] During the decade of the Cultural Revolution, schooling shut down nationwide, but beginning in the late 1970s entrance exams returned and schooling rapidly expanded. In the last two decades, China quickly rebuilt its education system in a process that paralleled those of Taiwan and South Korea in the 1960s. By the early 2000s a modern school system had emerged, although large urban-rural differences remain. Before 1980 few teachers were fully prepared. It took China over a decade to staff all schools with professionally trained teachers, only reaching the university level in the early 2000s. Since the 1990s private schooling has expanded. High-cost, elite private schools in cities serve the children of China's new rich. Other private schools, often at the primary level, have appeared in rural areas where fees for "public" schools can be high. An estimated twelve hundred new private universities have opened in recent years. Enrollments in Chinese universities have skyrocketed; the years 2005 to 2010 saw a 35 percent increase in university enrollment, nearly double the number of students that attended in 2000. This rapid growth raises questions about quality, and many new college graduates cannot find jobs.[18]

School-to-Work Linkages

Historically, East Asia closely connected school to work. Taiwan, South Korea, and Japan first expanded vocational high schools to prepare students for specific occupations. Major companies forged close ties to the specific universities from which they hired students. In pre-1980 China, the government assigned graduates to work units. The school-to-work link is evident in East Asia's success in producing college graduates in scientific fields, especially engineering, with the engineering emphasis continuing at the PhD level (See table 4.2). Although students may choose a college major, government influence over the secondary school curriculum, entrance exams, and university expansion have combined to direct students toward the fields most closely tied to national economic goals.

According to educational researcher William Cummings (1997), the Confucian tradition alone does not explain East Asian education. Rather,

Table 4.2. Percentage of University Graduates in a STEM Field, Including Engineering (2008)

Country	Four-Year College Degree		Doctoral Degree	
	Engineering	Other STEM	Engineering	Other STEM
China	31%	51%	25%	51%
Japan	17%	61%	24%	46%
South Korea	24%	41%	24%	40%
Taiwan	24%	40%	40%	64%
United States	4%	31%	13%	54%
Australia	7%	27%	15%	58%
Canada	7%	38%	18%	70%
United Kingdom	6%	34%	13%	57%

Note: STEM = science, technology, engineering, and mathematics, including the social sciences. Source: Appendix tables 2–33 and 2–35, National Science Foundation, Science and Engineering Indicators, 2012, http://www.nsf.gov/statistics/seind12/appendix.htm#c2 (accessed on January 26, 2014).

East Asian governments have followed a "J-Model" of education based on Japan's developmental path and response to western dominance.[19] Instead of advancing Confucian moral leadership, they mimic state-led rapid technological-industrial modernization to address international competition. The J-Model includes support for universal primary education that incorporates moral teaching, minimal public financing for advanced schooling (shifting the financial burden to families), and an emphasis on the science and engineering fields. National priorities shape secondary- and tertiary-level schooling while parents and the private sector must finance and supply much of the expanded schooling. Schooling both reinforces national economic development goals and protects nationalist values. This description explains why East Asia produces many engineers, why families invest heavily in schooling, and how rapid economic growth occurred while maintaining social stability.

After a person finishes school, full-time work starts in his or her early twenties. Retirement might be in a person's late fifties. East Asia has a low retirement age because employers want to reduce seniority-linked wage and benefit costs and create openings for energetic younger workers who possess new skills. The mandatory retirement age was sixty until recently but is now moving toward sixty-five years of age. Longer life expectancy combined with small pensions is forcing many in the retired population to rely on personal savings and part-time low-paying jobs for survival in their retirement years.

CONCLUSION

In 1950 East Asia's economies were in ruins, social life was in tatters, and nearly half the people were illiterate everywhere but Japan. Sixty plus years later the economies are strong, societies are vibrant, and schoolchildren top international achievement tests. A major factor explaining East Asia's transformation has been a sustained, intense commitment to schooling by parents and governments. In this chapter you learned about East Asian schooling and its contrasts with that in the United States. Americans claim to value education, to expect hard work for success, and to live in a competitive, merit-based society. Compared to the United States, schooling occupies a more central place in the lives of East Asians; commands greater parental and student attention; entails more competitive, merit-based outcomes; and is more closely tied to adult career advancement. Some people claim that America's great diversity, compared to East Asian's homogeneity, accounts for the differences in schooling and achievement. In the next chapter we examine diversity and inequality in East Asia.

INEQUALITY AND DIVERSITY IN EAST ASIA

Inequality and diversity take many forms. The social theorist Max Weber talked about class, status and power inequalities; economists examine income and wealth inequalities; geographers highlight urban-rural disparities; while sociologists discuss race-ethnicity, class and gender differences. The forms of inequality overlap. The economically poor, politically powerless and socially marginalized people are at the bottom and the wealthy, politically powerful and dominant social-cultural groups are at the top of society. In this chapter, you will learn about four forms of East Asian inequality-diversity: race-ethnic, gender, social class, and rural-urban.

RACIAL-ETHNIC DIVERSITY

Most Americans view East Asians as belonging to a single "Asian" racial group. Few in Asia see things this way, except when they interact with outsiders (e.g., Europeans or Africans). Instead, they identify with a country, e.g., Chinese or Korean, or an Asian ethnic group e.g., Okinawan or Tibetan.

South Korea

Korea, one of the world's most homogeneous societies, is fast becoming multicultural. For decades Koreans left their country in search of opportunity, and today nearly 7 million live outside Korea. Yet starting in the 1990s, the flow reversed, and immigration into South Korea accelerated. By 2010 about 2.5 percent of Korea's population was non-Korean. Officials expect this to grow to 5 percent by 2020 and 9.2 percent by 2050. Korea is now home to 20,000 second- or third-generation Chinese, 540,000 temporary foreign workers (over 90 percent unskilled), and 124,000 foreign brides.

Since the 1990s, foreign workers have migrated from low-wage countries to economically booming Korea. Most are males from Indonesia, the Philippines, Sri Lanka, Thailand, or Vietnam. In 2012 Korea's government began to scan the fingerprints and faces of entering foreigners to monitor this fast-growing, often undocumented, immigrant population.[1]

Foreign brides from China, Mongolia, the Philippines, and Vietnam were 11 percent of all Korean newlyweds in 2010. Their average age was twenty-three, versus forty-two for the Korean males they married. Korean males sought foreign mates because of a large sex ratio imbalance (more males than females). Also, after large numbers of Korean women acquired a college education, most wanted an urban lifestyle that would provide opportunities, and they avoided marrying the less-educated, older rural males. Korea's rising standard of living attracts the foreign brides. Unfortunately, many experience domestic abuse and misunderstanding. New Korean laws signal a greater acceptance of foreigners.[2]

Taiwan

Over 80 percent of all people in Taiwan are "Taiwanese," either Hokkien (also called Minnan) or Hakka. These Chinese ethnic groups speak non-Mandarin dialects and have distinct customs. They migrated long ago from the southern provinces of Fujian and Guangdong, respectively. The next largest group (13 to 14 percent of the population) is descended from 1.5 million Chinese nationalists who fled to Taiwan in 1949 after their defeat in China's civil war. Arriving shortly after the Japanese colonialists departed, the mainlanders took control, established a nondemocratic government, and imposed Mandarin (the official dialect of China) and northern Chinese, Han customs. As Taiwan's new economic and political elite, they held over half of all high government and business positions through the 1980s. Over the past thirty years, their mainlander identity has weakened and local Taiwanese people have gained a greater voice.[3]

Taiwan is also home to a collection of aboriginal peoples in nine groups (about 2 percent of the population) who have lived on the island for thousands of years. Residing in remote mountain areas, they retain distinct customs, languages, and religious beliefs. Until the late 1980s, they faced harsh discrimination and forced cultural assimilation. Their education and income levels are lower than those of the general population.[4]

Last, about six hundred thousand immigrants have entered Taiwan since the late 1990s. Most came from Southeast Asia (Indonesia, the Philippines, or Vietnam) or rural mainland China. About one-half are male "guest workers" who provide low-skill labor (e.g., construction, janitorial, or factory work) for Taiwan's booming economy. The rest are foreign brides. As in South Korea, foreign brides from low-income countries marry older, less-educated males. In 2010, 13 percent of all marriages were between a foreign bride and a Taiwanese man, a decline from nearly one in three in 2003. The brides face local resentment, especially if they come from mainland China, and they have high divorce rates.[5]

Japan

For a long time, Japan promoted an image of racial-ethnic homogeneity that overshadowed its demographic reality. As Japan expanded territorially in the nineteenth century, it conquered or absorbed peoples on its frontiers who had distinct languages, religions, and cultures. To the north Japan absorbed the Ainu, an indigenous people somewhat similar to American Indians. Over time most Ainu died, intermarried, or assimilated. Today about 30,000 pure Ainu remain, although 300,000 people may have some Ainu ancestry. To the south Japan conquered and absorbed the Ryūkyū kingdom's island chain, best known for its largest island, Okinawa. Okinawa's people did not attain equal legal rights as Japanese until 1920. During the Second World War, Japan turned Okinawa into a major military outpost. In a final major battle against the United States, Japan's army sacrificed Okinawa's civilians to protect the "pure Japanese" on the home island, Honshū. One-third of the civilian population died. For two decades after U.S. Occupation ended, the United States continued to control Okinawa, limiting local self-rule. Today 1.2 million Okinawans live on their home islands and 300,000 in the rest of Japan. Their income and education levels are below the Japanese average, and they face discrimination on Japan's main island. However, separation in a distant prefecture facilitated the preservation of a distinct language and ethnic identity.[6]

About one million people on Japan's main island, Honshū, are *burakumin* (hamlet people). They are descendants of the untouchable caste of pre-Meiji Japan. Although they are not physically different from other Japanese, mainstream Japanese view them as a separate racial-ethnic group. Identified by tracing their ancestry using family name and place of residence in Japan's *koseki* system, they once faced serious discrimination and were restricted to slums and low-skill, "unclean" occupations (e.g., garbage collection, leather tanning). A *burakumin* political movement fought for equal rights and antidiscrimination laws and eventually won improved conditions about forty years ago. Yet even today their income and education levels remain far below Japan's national average.[7]

Table 5.1. Japanese Minority Groups

Minority Group	Est. Number	Status	Origin
Ainu	30,000–300,000	Indigenous people, legal citizens	Nineteenth-century territorial expansion
Burakumin	1–3 million	"Untouchable" caste, legal citizens	Eighteenth century Tokugawa caste system
Zainichi, Korean or Taiwanese	750,000	Permanent Resident alien	Early-twentieth century colonial empire
Newcomer foreigners, *nikkeijin*	2.2 million	Foreigner, non citizens	Late-twentieth century globalization
Okinawans	1.2 million	Indigenous people, legal citizens	Nineteenth-century territorial expansion

Sources: Data are from Judicial System and Research Department, Minister's Secretariat, Ministry of Justice of the Japanese government and Weiner (2009).

Note: The largest groups among newcomer foreigners (as of 2009, latest data available) are 680,000 Chinese, 578,000 Koreans, 267,000 Brazilians, 211,000 Filipinos, 53,000 Americans and 51,000 Peruvians: http://www.stat.go.jp/english/data/nenkan/1431-02.htm (accessed on January 26, 2014).

When Korea and Taiwan were Japan's colonies, large numbers of Koreans (and some Taiwanese) moved to Japan as forced labor. By the end of the Second World War, two million Koreans were living in Japan. When a 1952 treaty revoked their Japanese citizenship, they legally became foreigners. About half returned to Korea, but the rest remained. Koreans who remained, known as *zainichi* (meaning "residing in Japan"), had to register as foreign aliens and lacked voting rights, even after living in Japan for three generations. To avoid harsh discrimination, many hid their Korean identities, adopted Japanese names, and spoke only Japanese in public. Divided between North and South Korean supporters, the *zainichi*'s income and education levels are below the national average. During the past fifteen years, pride in being Korean has spread, and Korean-Japanese intermarriage has increased.[8]

Excluding the *zainichi*, Japan's foreigner population grew from 118,000 in 1980 to 2.2 million in 2008. Nearly 300,000 are *nikkeijin*, (literally a "person with ties to Japan"). Most are people of Japanese origin who migrated to Brazil or Peru in the early twentieth century and returned in the 1980s when Japan had a labor shortage. They received favorable immigration treatment because they had "Japanese blood." Most took blue-collar factory jobs. Despite their Japanese ancestry, few were fluent in Japanese and most had adopted some Latin American customs. As a result friction developed with Japanese who expected the *nikkeijin* to speak and behave just like native Japanese.[9]

Last, Japan's foreign bride situation parallels those of Taiwan and South Korea. It represents about 5 percent of all Japanese marriages. The Philippines is the primary source of Japanese foreign brides, most whom marry rural men. Some local rural governments have organized "matchmaking" tours to the Philippines so unmarried males can meet prospective brides.[10]

China

Unlike its neighbors, China has long defined itself as a multiethnic country. Its empire included many minority peoples. In 1912 China's first president, Sun Yat-sen, called China a multiethnic country with five peoples (Han, Manchu, Mongolian, Tibetan, and Hui or Muslim). During conflicts between the communists and nationalists in the 1930s and 1940s, the Chinese Community Party revolutionaries lived among "minority peoples" in remote mountain regions and sought their support and protection. After the 1949 revolution, the CCP regime recognized ethnic-racial diversity and promised minority people autonomy.

China's term *minzu*, meaning "nationality group," comes from the Japanese word *minzuko*, "folk or ethnic group." In the 1950s China sought to classify all *minzu*. Initially, four hundred groups submitted applications, but the government accepted only fifty-four, plus the dominant Han group. Later this became fifty-five minorities, plus the majority Han. Officials applied criteria for *minzu* adopted from the Soviet Union: a

Figure 5.1. Minority Bai in traditional dress (Author photo).

71

Figure 5.2. Muslim boys in China (Author photo).

common territory, common language, shared economic system, and psychological identification. Officially recognized *minzu* receive limited political autonomy and some protection of their cultures.[11]

The fifty-five minority ethnic groups represent 9 percent of China's population and range from the Zhuang, with 16 million people, to eighteen others with over 1 million, and seven with under 10,000. Official categories combine some distinct minorities, creating tension. Many minority groups reside in China's strategic border regions or near natural resource or mineral deposits. Ten minorities are Muslim (Hui) that started as traders from China's west. Geographically scattered and without a common language, culture, or economy in the nineteenth century, the Hui gained cohesion and some now resist China's national government.[12]

After China's market reforms, education and income gaps grew between the majority Han and minorities. Most minorities reside in remote mountains or western China, while the Han are concentrated in the booming coastal cities. Many minorities fear "opening" their lands for natural resource exploitation and a large-scale in-migration of the Han that could weaken their cultural identity and autonomy. To lessen social division,

China's government exempts minorities from the one-child policy and provides preference in school access. The government highlights aspects of minority culture (e.g., customs, music, or clothing) but downplays the economic and political divisions. The national government's policies with regard to the Tibetan minority, because Tibet was once a separate country, has spawned periodic conflicts and become a source of political tension.[13]

GENDER INEQUALITY

East Asian gender stereotypes are widespread (e.g. males dominate while females are restricted "inside persons" who must walk behind males). In the twenty-first century, gender equality has grown, yet important variation remains by country and in the areas of pay, job equality, and attitudes.

The gender pay gap varies by country (see table 5.2). East Asia and the United States have larger gaps than the average for all advanced industrial democracies (most are European). It is largest in South Korea, where the typical male earns 38.9 percent more than a female, followed by Japan. The gap in China and Taiwan is less than that of the United States. Over the past twenty years, the gender pay gap has remained stable in South Korea, declined in Japan and Taiwan, and grown in China.

Several factors contribute to a gender pay gap: overt discrimination, differences in education, part- versus full-time work, promotion opportu-

Table 5.2. The Gender Pay Gap, 2009

Country	Gender Pay Gap (% average male pay exceeds average female pay)
China	17.5
Japan	28.9
South Korea	38.9
Taiwan	17.9
United States	19.8
Average of 26 OECD Countries	15.8

Sources: For the OECD data, Chart LMF1.5.A, Gender Gap in Median Earnings of Full-Time Employees, 2009, www.oecd.org/dataoecd/1/35/43199347.xls (accessed on January 26, 2014). For the non-OECD data, Tsai 2012 for Taiwan and Su and Heshmati 2011 for China.

nities, gender concentration by industry or occupation, and family division of labor. Across East Asia, the pay gap is smaller for unmarried than married women with children. This suggests that gender differences in family obligations are a major contributing factor.[14]

Cultural beliefs that reinforce unequal gender roles vary by country and are strongest in Japan. As you read in the last chapter, until recently few Japanese women completed four years of college. In South Korea women attend four-year colleges at rates equal to men, but large gender differences remain in college majors and many university-educated women use their degrees more to attract husbands than for career preparation. In Japan married women often work part time. Countries also vary by whether women advance to managerial positions (see table 5.3).[15]

China presents a more complex picture. During the Maoist era, pay was equal by gender; however, as the market economy spread and the government adopted a "hands-off" policy, gender inequality has increased. China's gender pay gap was about 5 percent in the 1980s, 15 percent in the 1990s, and 25 percent in the early 2000s. It has continued to accelerate since 2002. With the transition to a market economy, more women than men have remained in low-paying state sector jobs or nonmanagerial occupations. Men, more than women, have moved to high-paying private sector jobs. The most advanced, private market areas of China's economy have the largest gender pay gaps. Recent urban migrants have a larger gender pay gap compared to established residents. As sociologists Philip Cohen and Feng Wang (2009, 51) noted, "Post-socialist economic reforms in China have resulted in a clear reversal of one of the proudest accomplishments under socialism: pay equity between female and male urban employees."[16]

CHINA'S "MISSING GIRLS"

Missing girls refers to an unbalanced sex ratio at birth (i.e., number of males per 100 females). Since the 1980s recorded male births have exceeded what should occur naturally. In 1989 it was close to normal (105 males per 100 females) for first births, but it became more unbalanced with each additional child: 121:100 for second child, 125:100 for third child, and 132:100 for fourth child. By 2000 the overall sex ratio was 120:100, the most unbalanced in the world. Based the natural birth ratio, this translates into about 14 girls "missing" for each 120 recorded male births.

A strong cultural preference for males and China's one-child policy aggravate the birth sex ratio imbalance. Four factors explain it: high death

Table 5.3. Characteristics of Working Women in Three East Asian Countries

Country	% in Professional Positions	% in Managerial Positions	% in Temporary, Part-Time Positions
Japan	46	10	36
South Korea	38	7	8
Taiwan	44	16	6

Source: Chang and England 2010.

rates for female babies through infanticide, neglect, or abandonment; the underreporting of female births; mostly girls put up for adoption; and sex-selective abortions. Female infanticide is illegal, but families hide female births from the authorities so they can try again to have a son. Many adoptions are unrecorded or unofficial; however, most adoptions are of abandoned infant girls. Ultrasound machines spread in China in the 1990s. Using them for sex-selective births is illegal, but the sex of a fetus is not recorded and for-profit private clinics own many of the machines. The cumulative effective is serious. Estimates put the single male population unable to find a wife at thirty million by 2017 with rural "bachelor villages" appearing. The government is aware of the issue and hopes to address birth sex ratio imbalance.[17]

SOCIAL CLASS AND ECONOMIC INEQUALITY

It is easy to confuse four overlapping and connected ideas: economic inequality, occupation, social class, and social mobility. Let us look at each one separately.

Economic inequality refers to the distribution, or top-to-bottom spread, of an economic resource such as income (e.g., wages or salaries) or wealth (owning land, buildings, or investment stocks and bonds). Rich versus poor and poverty rates describe economic inequality.

Occupation refers to a type of job (e.g., accountant, investment banker, police officer, waitress, business owner, plumber, or schoolteacher). An occupation requires certain skills and schooling, and it provides levels of job security, work conditions, and pay. Job security, work conditions, and pay can vary based on type and relative size of employer (e.g., small business versus a large multinational corporation). Overall changes in the economy cause some occupations to expand in size and others to decline.

Social class refers to ranked categories of families that share a similar level of social and economic resources. People with the same occupation tend to be in the same class (e.g., factory workers are working class). Besides economic resources, social class members often share a similar lifestyle, view of the world, and cultural tastes (e.g., opera versus NASCAR). They also tend to marry one another. Instead of social class, some people use socioeconomic status, a numerical measure that combines level of income, years of schooling, and occupational prestige rank.

Social mobility refers to changes in class position, usually from parents to child. Despite all the publicity, significant class mobility from one generation to another is rare. Most people remain in the same class as their parents. Parents with substantial financial and educational resources try to ensure that their children will remain in the same class and not slide downward. Many parents push their children to try to move upward in the class hierarchy. In any era the level of inequality, mix of occupations, size of social classes, and degree of movement across class lines can vary by country.

You may have heard that the United States is more unequal than other industrialized nations, and that inequality has grown over the past twenty-five years. East Asia had low levels of economic inequality in the 1980s, but this has increased across East Asia. Changes in Japan and China led to dramatic changes in inequality, class, and mobility.

Japan

In the 1980s Japan had a roaring economy, a low level of income inequality, and unemployment and poverty rates that were near zero. Young people moved seamlessly from school to full-time work, many joining Japan's "lifetime" employment system. Today Japan looks very different. After two decades of nearly stagnant economic growth, inequality and unemployment have grown, and youths struggle to start a stable, full-time career. During the 1990s economic downturn, Japan's companies retained their middle-aged employees, most who, would retire in their late fifties. They switched from hiring new full-time career people to largely hiring part-time and temporary workers. Young adults bore the brunt of this restructuring, and the school-to-work system unraveled.

A "lost generation" emerged in Japan comprised of "parasite singles," *furiita*, and NEETs. A parasite single is a twenty- to thirty-five-year-old who remains unmarried, lives with her or his parents, holds a low-level job, and spends most earnings on clothing, travel, and entertainment. The word *furiita* joins the Japanese pronunciation of *free* with the term for part-time worker, *arubaito*. It refers to young adults in part-time, temporary, noncareer jobs that they frequently switch. The Japanese Ministry of Health, Labor, and Welfare coined the term NEET ("Not in Education, Employment, or Training") to describe persons age fifteen to thirty-five who are not married, not in school, and not employed (or looking for work).[18]

Before the 1990s most Japanese high school graduates continued on to university or found full-time work. Today about 20 percent are NEETs. In some high schools, half of graduates are NEETs. Increasingly, teens from low-prestige high schools begin to work at low-pay, part-time jobs while still in school. After graduating they continue through a string of similar low-pay, "dead-end" jobs for a decade or more. Conservative Japanese leaders have blamed young people for being immature and spoiled, and for refusing to accept the responsibility of marriage and a serious career. Social scientists see the rising age of marriage and unstable job situation as less of a "free choice" than the result of restructured adult labor markets.

After twenty years of near stagnant economic growth and intensified global competition, low-wage, temporary service sector jobs replaced many of Japan's once well-paying, stable, blue-collar and white-collar jobs. A postindustrial economy emerged. It has a few high-end, well-paid professional careers, a huge number of unstable, low-end service jobs, and some stable midlevel jobs. Japan is not unique in transitioning to a postindustrial economy; however, the transition happened very fast and disrupted a once highly effective system that ensured most young men stable, full-time employment. For decades Japanese females formed a large part-time, temporary labor force with few career prospects. Now Japan's young males are finding themselves in the same situation.

Japan's entire occupational-class system is in transition. Social mobility and movement across class lines were common in the 1960s–80s. This has slowed, social divisions have solidified, and intergenerational class differences are growing. Youths are not alone. A large homeless population is now evident in Japanese city parks. Japan combines an early retirement age (fifty-five to sixty), meager pensions, and limited social welfare services. Many men who held low-level, blue-collar jobs and lack family support or enough savings, find themselves destitute.[19]

Figure 5.3. Homeless settlement in
a Tokyo park (Author photo).

South Korea and Taiwan industrialized later and experienced more moderate restructuring. Economic inequality increased in both countries, but compared to Japan, inequality increased only moderately. Both are transitioning toward a postindustrial economy, but neither had to dismantle an effective, tightly integrated, and inflexible employment system like that of Japan and both largely avoided the degree of disruption that produced Japan's "lost generation." Survey data (see table 5.4) show Japanese pessimism. The 2010 results are an improvement over pessimism levels for Japan in 2002, when 12 percent were satisfied and 6 percent said Japan had a good economy.

Table 5.4. Four-Nation Comparison: Optimistic, Satisfied, and Good Economic Situation (2010)

Country	% Optimistic about the Future	% Satisfied with Society	% Saying Economy Is Good
China	74	87	91
Japan	32	20	12
South Korea	65	21	18
United States	52	30	24

Source: Pew Global Attitudes 2010: www.pewglobal.org/question-search/ (accessed on January 26, 2014). *Note*: Survey questions were about people feeling generally optimistic about the future, overall satisfaction with society, and feeling that the economic situation was somewhat good or very good.

China

As table 5.4 shows, most Chinese are satisfied and optimistic. This is despite great increases in economic inequality. Before 1980 China ranked as lowest in economic inequality; today it is among the world's most unequal countries. Living conditions and social benefits (e.g., housing, health care, and schooling) also became unequal. Thirty years ago all Chinese had relatively equal benefits; today some get nothing while others have excellent benefits.

China had seventy-seven billionaires in U.S. dollars as of 2008 (latest data available). At the same time, nearly one-third of the population struggles to earn two dollars per day; however, this is a huge improvement over 1996, when nearly two-thirds earned that little. Change in China is more complex than the transition from a command-socialist to a market-capitalist economy. Elements of the old system remain, especially for the 5 percent of the population who are CCP members. China has a hybrid economy in which some leading "private" companies are actually under government control.[20] As social demographer Feng Wang (2008, 50) summarized it, "Together with changes in the political system that drastically reduced the importance of political participation in daily life, the new economic system emerging during this time led to a fundamental reconfiguration of Chinese society, altering the role of the state and local governments, work organizations, and the family organization in individuals' social and economic lives."

Personal income has increased in China but at very different rates in different places. Inequality varies by geographic area, firm or work unit, sector, and rural-urban location. Economic inequality in China differs from that found in the United States by region and work unit. Across cities inequality is modest in the United States. In the United States a person in one city earns an income similar (usually no more than two or three times more) to that of a person with a similar job and experience elsewhere, but large income differences exist among people within the same city (some earn twenty to thirty times more). In the 1980s urban China matched the U.S. pattern; however, by 1995 inequality across cities had grown. Some cities prospered and most residents benefited, and the gap between them and people in the "falling behind" cities dramatically increased. A parallel difference occurs among firms. Within-firm inequality in the United States can be huge; the chief executive officer might earn seventy times more than the average worker does. Yet people working in the same occupation (e.g., engineer) in different firms tend to have similar incomes. China has small within-firm inequality but large across-firm inequality. For example, the most highly paid Chinese executive might earn six times or more than the average worker does, but people with the same occupation (such as engineers) working in different firms may be paid very differently (e.g., twenty-five times more in one firm than in another). In the United States, inequality mostly operates across individuals, while in China inequality mostly operates across cities and work units.

A *danwei* is a work unit in a retail business, school, hospital, government agency, or factory. This unique Chinese institution evolved from self-sufficient units the CCP created in the 1930s–40s. *Danwei* grew in power in the 1950s, when China copied a Soviet Union factory model that integrated the industrial work unit with social benefits (e.g., housing, health care, education, etc.). As the Stanford University sociologist Xueguang Zhou (2004, 102) explained, "[T]he role of work organizations has attained a prominent role that is unprecedented historically and unrivaled in other societies, partly due to the importance of such organizations in resource allocation and partly due to restrictions on job mobility."

During the Maoist era, each *danwei* was a self-contained society in urban China (collective farms operated in rural areas). It provided a worker and his or her family with housing, food, schooling, health care, recreational facilities, and a pension. Wages declined in importance since a *danwei* provided for most needs. Transferring between *danwei* was nearly impossible, and most new hires were relatives of current members. In addition to being a critical economic and social unit, the *danwei* monitored political loyalty to the CCP. It controlled what a person could read and where he or she could travel.[21]

The *danwei* did not disappear with China's market reforms. As late as 1985, *danwei* still owned 35 percent of all of China's urban housing and over one-fourth of all hospital beds. Early in the reform era, some *danwei* expanded, reinvested their earnings, and branched out into new industries; they became wealthy and improved worker living conditions. Other *danwei* fell behind. By the early 2000s, *danwei* weakened as job choice and privately purchased housing and medical care spread. Yet even today large private Chinese factories typically provide their employees with housing and other services.[22]

During the Maoist era, China had a state-socialist redistribution system. It followed a political logic rather than the market logic of the capitalist-market system we find elsewhere in East Asia and in the United

States. Under the political logic, a person's party membership, *danwei*, and shifting national political policies dictated residence, job, pay, and promotion prospects, not one's talent, skills, or effort. Starting in 1978 reforms created a fundamental break in work life, economic activity, and social stratification. A "dual career path model" emerged. In it a person advanced in a career primarily based on his or her individual merit or his or her political loyalty and connections. The professional-technical staff advanced based on merit, while the managerial-administrative staff had a basic level of education but advanced largely based on political loyalty.[23]

During the Maoist era, almost the entire urban population worked in the state enterprises or collectives overseen by local governments; private sector employment was nearly zero. With market reform, private sector employment grew to 13 percent by 1994. Eight years later, in 2002, over one-half of the urban population worked in the private sector (see table 5.5). In less than a generation, China went from everyone working for the government to a majority of urban people working in the private, for-profit sector.[24]

URBAN-RURAL INEQUALITY

East Asia's major cities (Tokyo, Seoul, Taipei, and Shanghai) had the best jobs and the greatest educational, health care, and cultural opportunities. During 1970s–80s era rapid economic growth, millions migrated from rural areas to cities in Japan, South Korea, and Taiwan, and now a majority (80

Table 5.5. Urban Employment in China by Sector

Year	% in State Sector	% in Collectives	% in Private Sector
1952	63.5	1	35.5
1970	76	22.5	1.5 (peak of Maoist era)
1990	70	24	6.0
1994	67	20	13
2000	54	10	36
2006	29	4	67

Source: Frazier (2006) and Szamosszegi and Kyle (2011).

Figure 5.4. A house in rural China (Author photo).

percent) of people in these countries reside in large cities. The depopulated rural villages and small towns are now filled with the elderly. They offer few job opportunities, low incomes, and limited schooling.

China is East Asia's least urban society, and it has the world's biggest rural-urban gap. In 1950, 87 percent of China's population lived in rural villages. This declined to 82 percent in 1970 and 74 percent in 1990. The rural decline accelerated, from 64 percent rural in 2001 to 56 percent in 2007. By 2015 China's urban population will exceed its rural population for the first time in history.

Policies of the Maoist era intensified China's rural and urban division, creating one form of socialism for the countryside and another for urban areas. Rural people lived in "socialist serfdom," unable to leave or to sell products openly; they had to supply a quota of agricultural goods to the government at fixed, low prices. The *hukou* system (discussed in chapter 3) prevented people from leaving rural areas and helped people in cities where the government invested heavily in industry.[25]

Since 1978, market reforms have opened new opportunities in rural areas. By 2000, 30 percent of rural people were supplementing their farm incomes by earning private sector wages. Despite improvements in rural areas, rapid economic growth in cities has produced large urban-rural gaps in income, educational levels, and living standards.[26] The benefits of market reform spread unevenly. Some private individuals without CCP connections became entrepreneurs and started new businesses; however, many CCP leaders and their relatives became private entrepreneurs and began earning high incomes. Thus, market reforms often failed to eliminate the power of CCP cadres or to replace them with private, capitalist entrepreneurs. Rather, many CCP cadres have combined their political positions with additional resources from an expanding capitalist-market economy to become "Red capitalists."

In addition many of China's private entrepreneurs embrace continued nondemocratic CCP rule rather that supporting a shift to a multiparty open democracy. They have forged alignments with CCP officials who promise to protect their business interests. The CCP recruits wealthy entrepreneurs into the party, and many entrepreneurs want to join the CCP.[27]

Spreading market reforms and a loosening of the *hukou* system created a third major social group between the rural and urban populations: illegal rural migrants in cities. By the 1990s millions of people were migrating from impoverished rural areas to China's booming coastal cities. Yet few could get legal *hukou* permission to resettle. Officials grant resettlement

Figure 5.5. A luxury apartment building in Beijing (Author photo).

permission only to people with a high level of education or a high post in the CCP. Such permission provides access to all urban services, such as housing, health care, and schooling. Few poor rural migrants can secure *hukou* permission.

Millions have traveled great distances and risked penalties for an opportunity to earn far more than they could in rural areas. This "floating population" of illegal migrants is mostly young (under thirty) and unmarried. They work construction jobs or in factories, under harsh conditions such as twelve-hour workdays and six- or seven-day workweeks, and live in packed factory dormitories where ten or twelve people might share a tiny room, sleeping on triple bunk beds. Their low wages (e.g., fifty cents an hour) are a great improvement over what they were able to earn in rural areas. As illegal migrants, they lack access to schools, health care, and other services. Local officials treat them as unruly second-class citizens and see them as a drain on urban resources. Estimates place China's floating population at 150 million people. This varies by area. In Shanghai 30 percent of the population is floating population migrants; elsewhere it is as high as 78 percent.[28]

Over the thirty years since the end of the Maoist era, China has become one of the world's most economically unequal societies. The Chinese people recognize the growing inequality, but few see it as unjust. Many say there is too much inequality and object to inequality that comes from political connections and personal connections (*guanxi*) or that ignores the basic needs of the infirm, elderly, and extremely poor. Most also believe the *hukou* system is unfair. Yet the Chinese embrace merit-based market competition and understand that it generates inequality. China's most disadvantaged people (e.g., low-wage workers and farmers) have seen dramatic real gains in material conditions over the past two decades, and they remain optimistic about the future and their chances for upward mobility.

China's dramatic increase in inequality has not produced a "social volcano" of widespread unrest. Only limited unrest has erupted around specific issues (e.g., extreme pollution and failure to provide disaster relief). The CCP regime has largely upheld its social-political legitimacy. The Chinese more than Americans or the Japanese believe that hard work produces rewards (61 percent in China vs. 37 percent in the United States and 16 percent in Japan) and that government officials care about ordinarily people (50 percent in China vs. 43 percent in the United States and 25 percent in Japan). The post-Maoist reforms have increased job mobility within and between firms and allowed advancement based on merit; nonetheless, *guanxi* and corruption through political connections remain important impediments.[29]

CONCLUSION

Thirty years ago East Asian societies were among the world's most economically equal and least socially diverse. Since then economic inequality and social diversity have grown, though at different rates and in different ways.[30] The shift to a global, postindustrial economy that triggers economic restructuring explains rising inequality in Japan, South Korea, and Taiwan, and the shift from a command-socialist to a market economy explains growing inequality in China. In the next and last chapter, we look forward to the forces that may shape East Asian societies in the next thirty years.

LOOKING TO THE FUTURE

I n this last chapter, we look at the future and consider four issues: economic growth, globalization, societal adjustment, and nationalism.

ECONOMIC GROWTH

Economic growth means that a society produces more goods and services this year than last year. Economists measure it as a percentage increase. Sustained growth rates of over 6 percent per year for ten or more years are rare and have only occurred three times in recorded history: Japan had an 8 percent growth rate from 1955 to 1973, and South Korea and Taiwan had 7 percent growth rates from 1982 to 1996. China has had a growth rate of 7 percent from 1978 to the present, and the rate exceeded 9 percent each year between 2002 and 2011. In a global perspective, East Asia is noteworthy for such rapid economic growth.[1] Economies are so dynamic, especially across East Asia, that it is not easy to make accurate predictions of future trends. Nevertheless, recent developments can help us to envision future directions.

As you have learned, East Asia was devastated after the Second World War, so scholars have sought to explain these "economic miracles." They have attributed it to a combination of Confucian values, new economic growth policies, geopolitical alignments of the era, and national institutions with close business-government alliances.[2]

We have already discussed Confucian values, so let us consider the role of new economic growth policies. During the 1950s, most less-developed countries followed an import-substitution policy to become self-sufficient and reduce their dependence on other countries. Under this policy, the national government imposed high tariffs to limit imported goods, and it encouraged domestic companies to "substitute," or supply, all products consumed within a country. The strategy sought to reduce the outflow of money for goods made outside the country and spur domestic industry. However, it resulted in high consumer prices for a limited range of domestic products that were rarely of top quality. After two decades, the import-substitution policy failed to ignite significant economic growth. This was for many reasons: a scarcity of materials or resources, small local markets, lack of access to the latest equipment or technology, and limited investment and competition.

Japan

Japan adopted something different; an export-led growth policy. This strategy focused on making products (e.g., autos, clothing, radios, televisions, or toys) to sell overseas. It successfully stimulated rapid economic growth in Japan in the 1960s and 1970s. South Korea and Taiwan followed the same strategy in the 1980s and 1990s, and China joined in by the 1990s and 2000s.[3]

Under an export-led growth strategy, domestic industries concentrate on foreign sales and learn to produce goods that meet international quality standards at competitive prices. One goal is to bring new revenue from overseas into a country. Government policies pressure private industry to reinvest the new revenue in upgrading worker training and skills, modernizing production processes with the latest equipment and technology, and shifting over time to exporting high-value, high-profit products. A country may start by exporting low-cost, labor-intensive products such as textiles (while paying low wages for low skilled labor), but over time it will move to making complex, sophisticated products such as computer chips or high-definition televisions, which require highly skilled labor and advanced technology.

Japan adopted an export-led growth strategy for several reasons. The United States assisted Japan's rapid economic rebuilding during the Korean War (1950–53) by asking it to produce supplies for the U.S. military. The United States wanted Japan to rebuild quickly to create a strong, stable, East Asian anticommunist ally during the Cold War. Later the United States began opening up its markets to goods imported from Japan. By the mid-1970s, American consumers could buy high-quality, low-cost Japanese products. Forced to readjust, American industry also grew stronger and more internationally competitive. In addition Japan kept the value of its currency, the yen, very low. This made Japanese products cheap for consumers in other countries. At the same time, goods imported into Japan were expensive and Japanese consumers paid high prices. Yet rapid economic growth had created new many jobs and eliminated unemployment in Japan.[4] Despite some differences, South Korea and Taiwan were also part of the U.S.–East Asian anticommunist geopolitical alliance and followed Japan's path (see below).

National institutions and close business-government alliances are other factors that supported East Asian development and an export-led growth strategy. Again Japan was in front. Chalmers Johnson in a 1982 book, *MITI and the Japanese Miracle*, outlined the developmental state model, also called state-led developmental capitalism. In the model, a strong national government

Figure 6.1. Japanese "bullet train," a symbol of economic success (Author photo).

with limited corruption recruits the country's most talented people to work at building a strong nation. The government designs an entire system of taxes, business regulations, investment incentives, public works, and labor policies that encourage export-led economic growth. Domestic companies reinvest their profits in innovation (rather than rewarding stockholders or paying high salaries to corporate officers), companies collaborate with one another (rather than intensely competing), and the government protects domestic markets from foreign competition (rather than giving consumers low prices and many choices). A government ministry targets certain industries for expansion and allows others to decline. In short government technocrats pick "winners and losers" and steer the economy to strengthen the nation. Besides an active, competent government bureaucracy, the model requires cooperation by major companies and business leaders.[5]

Japan's developmental state was in part a legacy of its strong, activist government before its defeat in 1945. A second pre-1945 legacy was a history of cooperation within Japan's highly concentrated industry and banking sectors. A handful of interconnected large companies and banks called *zaibatsu* had dominated Japan's pre-1945 economy. American Occupation officials first tried to dissolve the *zaibatsu* and encourage free market competition to promote democracy. However, they later backed off from the total dismantling of *zaibatsu* in order to speed Japan's rebuilding.

As Japan rebuilt in the 1950s, a weaker version of the *zaibatsu* developed; the *keiretsu*. Japan's powerful trade ministry (called MITI, or Ministry of International Trade and Industry, until 2001 when its name changed) worked closely with *keiretsu* to create an export-led national economy.

A *keiretsu* such as Mitsubishi is a tightly interconnected, cooperating company group involved in shipping, electronics, chemicals, banking, real estate, insurance, steel making, and cameras. *Keiretsu* produce many well-known Japanese brands (e.g., Sony, Fuji Film, Canon, Hitachi, Nikon, Sharp, Mazda, and Toyota). Member companies of a *keiretsu* invest in one another and buy one another's products; they operate as a single "supercompany." Thus, the *keiretsu* bank provides the *keiretsu* camera company with no-interest loans, the *keiretsu* real estate company assists in building new camera factories, the *keiretsu* shipping company charges ultra-low-cost shipping rates, and so forth.[6]

Some scholars see the developmental state as a significant alternative to the Anglo-American (also called neo-liberal) system of government-business relations.[7] In the "neoliberal" model, best represented by the United States, private investors (wealthy stockholders and investment bankers) not government planners make decisions in a loosely regulated market that shape the pace and direction of economic growth as they pursue profits. An ideal neo-liberal "free market" system allows entrepreneurs to enter the marketplace easily and to form and expand companies with a minimum of government oversight. In the neo-liberal model, "winners and losers" rise or fall based on an ability to satisfy consumers and to deliver profits. In theory, this model will generate economic growth in the long term, yet it lacks stability and tends to increase economic inequality.

The great success of East Asian economies in the 1970s and 1980s raised questions about the neo-liberal model. However, in the 1990s East Asian economies faced problems and a financial crisis, while the U.S. economy was booming. As a result, the neo-liberal model quickly returned to prominence and public attention shifted away from East Asia's developmental state/export-led growth system.[8]

South Korea and Taiwan

The United States also sought a strong anticommunist ally in South Korea during the Cold War. Less industrialized than Japan, Korea's economic advancement was delayed by at least a decade. American aid provided about 70 percent of imports 1953–61, then under a military dictatorship the government seized all banks and restructured government-business

Figure 6.2. Corporate logo (used since 2009) of LG, a South Korean holding company with over thirty companies worldwide involved in chemicals, consulting, electronics, real estate, professional sports, and telecom fields. Source: http://commons.wikimedia.org/wiki/File:LG_LOGO_NEW.jpg.

relations. As occurred in Japan, a combination of devalued currency, strong government direction, and high tariffs on foreign imports stimulated export-led growth. A small set of large integrated companies and banks, called *chaebol*, emerged under direct government aid and soon dominated South Korea's economy. These integrated firms (e.g., Samsung, Hyundai, and LG) differ somewhat from Japan's *keiretsu*. *Chaebol* only appeared in the 1960s, and they did grow out of pre-1950 firms. Korea's government-owned banks gave the *chaebol* extensive assistance. A single family owns a *chaebol* and occupies its top management positions. After the mid-1990s economic crisis, western pressures, and scandals over bribery and corruption, South Korea, like Japan, began moving in the direction of a neoliberal, free market economy.[9]

Taiwan also followed a developmental state model, but its economy, unlike those of Japan and South Korea, is largely comprised of small and medium-sized family-run businesses. American aid stabilized postwar Taiwan and provided over 30 percent of domestic investment from 1951 to 1962. The U.S. commitment weakened after President Nixon visited China in 1972, so Taiwan aggressively moved toward export-led growth. Taiwan's government encouraged a shift away from labor-intensive manufacturing and toward heavy industry in the 1970s, and then moved into advanced electronics (LCD screens and computer chips) during the 1980s and 1990s. In the 1990s policies again changed with greater democratization and mainland China's fast economic rise and market reforms. Banks and companies that had been under tight government control were privatized, and Taiwan's economy moved in a neoliberal direction. Japan, South Korea, and Taiwan all invest in factories across Asia, including China.

However, with a shared language and culture, Taiwanese business moved rapidly into mainland China. Over 80 percent of all Taiwan's overseas investment goes to China, and it controls 25 percent of all foreign-owned manufacturing in China.[10]

China

As in other areas, China dramatically differs from the rest of East Asia. The government ran a "command economy" with complete control over all economic activity until 1978 when it began to phase in features of market capitalism. In the 1980s, as China introduced market reforms and opened its economy to the outside world, it, too, adopted an export-led growth strategy. By the 1990s China had a hybrid "market socialism" economy with some large private companies. Its state development model with export-led growth differed from those of its capitalist neighbors. It began with total government ownership of the economy and advanced under the close supervision the one-party, nondemocratic Communist government. As the economist Thomas Palley (2006, 72) noted, "[E]xport production has been a core element of China's export-led growth strategy. In the absence of a developed domestic consumer market, China has relied on foreign markets—especially the US market—to provide demand for the goods produced by Chinese factories." He believes that China's export-led growth development model will be unsustainable in the future.

China's fast-growing economy is unbalanced in several ways: geographically, by economic sector, by environmental impact, and by social distribution. Over 90 percent of the population lives on half the country's land, mostly in eastern and coastal areas. The western half of China is dry, mountainous, and sparsely populated. The half of the population that lives in rural areas has experienced slower economic growth, and some rural areas are becoming depopulated as masses of people migrate to cities. In addition various economic sectors (e.g., accounting, agriculture, banking, electronics, housing, retail, and transportation) are not advancing equally fast. Such highly uneven development and serious corruption are not surprising given the speed of change. If the United States took 150 years to modernize and Japan accelerated the process to 75, China, with one-fifth of the world's population, is attempting to achieve similar change in under 50.[11] East Asia's developmental state model with export-led growth was successful for several decades. Yet its ability to sustain rapid growth indefinitely is an open question. Other countries are adopting the same growth strategy, and the overall global economy is changing.

GLOBAL CONNECTIONS

The terms *globalization* and *globalism* are only thirty years old, but they are now part of everyday language. For centuries people traveled long distances and exchanged goods and beliefs with one another. A qualitative change occurred over the past three decades as the speed, extent, and scope of connections across the globe greatly intensified. As the British political scientist David Held and his associates (1999, 2) noted, "Globalization may be thought of initially as the widening, deepening and speeding up of worldwide interconnectiveness in all aspects of contemporary social life, from the cultural to the criminal, from the financial to the spiritual." Communication, travel, and the exchange of ideas, goods, and money accelerated and spread in ways that never occurred previously.

Technological advances, changing economies, and new trade rules combined to create twenty-first-century globalization. We are most familiar with the technological changes (e.g., faster ships and planes, the Internet, and fiber optic phone lines) and postindustrial economies. International trade changed with new, worldwide agreements among countries. After the Second World War, about two dozen countries signed the General Agreement on Tariffs and Trade (GATT) to set global rules. Membership grew from 26 participating countries in 1960s to 123 by 1983. The framework expanded and became the World Trade Organization (WTO) in 1995. New rules made shipping products, moving money, and performing professional services across national borders much easier. When China joined the WTO in 2001, it was the 142nd member.[12] East Asia, with its export-led growth, has rapidly integrated into global relationships.

Beyond the technological and economic changes, globalization also affects the daily lives of the world's people. People are coming into increased contact with media, music, foods, and fashions that flow across international borders. They are encountering new ideas, different beliefs, and dissimilar cultural practices faster and more often than ever before. This can be both exciting and unsettling.

Globalization rearranges benefits and costs for people locally. People see benefits in the form of cheaper consumer products, a wider variety of goods and foods, novel and stimulating ideas, and new opportunities. They experience the costs as they encounter disturbing sounds, tastes, or smells; learn of unusual beliefs or social practices; see traditional forms of work disappear; and feel that established ways of doing things are being disrupted. While people have always adapted to change, the great speed of change intensifies both its costs and its benefits.

Figure 6.3. McDonalds in Tokyo. Source: http://commons.wikimedia. org/wiki/File:TokyoSetagayaMcDonalds.jpg.

Figure 6.4. KFC in China. Source: http://commons.wikimedia.org/wiki/ File:Kfc_in_siping.jpg.

Globalization's benefits and costs are unevenly distributed. Benefits primarily flow to the most adaptive, informed, well-connected people who possess high-value talents or skills. The costs are borne by less flexible or isolated people who lack special skills or talents. Thus, globalization is bringing people from around the world together, as its consequences are simultaneously dividing and separating people within and between countries.

Globalization has brought East Asia closer to America and elsewhere. East Asia touches many peoples' lives through its exports of products, services, ideas, and fashions. At the same time, foreign ideas, tastes, and beliefs are quickly flowing into East Asia. Globalization accelerates change everywhere, but rapid, recent modernization and dramatic economic growth in East Asia may have intensified globalization's impact there more than elsewhere. The great speed and impact of globalization on social life have required people to adapt and adjust quickly.

SOCIAL ADJUSTMENTS

Social conditions constantly change, and people learn to adjust, yet the dramatic and very rapid changes in East Asia across the past several decades demand significant social adjustments. Traditional East Asian family and gender relations, in which people had arranged marriages, lived in large multigenerational families, and accepted unquestioned male authority have been transformed in less than a generation. Today's young adults of both genders have many lifestyle choices and freedoms, are informed and educated, and are living in small families in urban settings. Most young East Asians study English in school and can taste dishes, watch films, and listen to music coming from elsewhere. Encounters between traditional culture and new conditions are not always without disruption.

One example illustrates such disruption and adjustment. Most East Asian societies have slow or declining overall population growth and a rapidly increasing elderly population. This is happening worldwide. However, in East Asia the traditional three-generation household is disappearing. As a result providing social and health care for a large elderly population has emerged as a major public issue. Rapid industrialization and urbanization are combined with increased life expectancy resulting from improved living standards.

More contentious than the issue of deciding how East Asian societies will provide and pay for elder services is the changing place of elders in society. Confucian beliefs upheld elders as revered sources of wisdom worthy of great respect. Today many of the elderly feel ignored, forgotten, and left behind. Likewise, traditional gender expectations were highly unequal. They, too, are changing fast, creating uncertainty with many choices and responsibilities that differ from those of the past.

One visible cost of East Asia's rapid economic and social change is its high elderly suicide rates. Compared to English-speaking countries, East Asian countries have higher general suicide rates, especially for women. Elderly suicide greatly exceeds that of the overall population (see table 6.1).

Table 6.1. Suicides among the Elderly

Country	Elderly Suicide Rate (per million)		Elderly Rate/General Population Rate for Each Gender[a]	
	Female	Male	Female	Male
Urban China	440	510	4.78	6.62
Rural China	932	1,327	3.14	5.85
Japan	412	569	3.95	2.62
South Korea	154	373	2.70	2.98
United States	56	507	1.24	2.56
Canada	46	280	0.83	1.33

Source: Pritchard and Baldwin 2002.

Note: Elderly is defined as a person seventy-five years or older.

[a] 1.0 means the elderly rate is the same as that of the general population.

For example, China's elderly are five or six times more likely to die by suicide than are its adults under seventy-five years of age. Social isolation and depression are common suicide causes everywhere, but East Asia's elderly may be experiencing a loss of past high status, admiration for their economic contributions and moral standards, and a secure place within the extended family.[13] Rapid economic and social changes also are disrupting gender relations.

In addition to elderly suicide rates, East Asia's rates of divorce, crime, and out-of-wedlock births have been rising in recent decades. These individual and family-level adjustment responses to a fast-changing society are broadly spreading to affect people's identities and political communities.

NATIONALISM AND NATIONAL IDENTITY

The nation is a significant unit for politics, society, and economy, and it is a basis for identity. Most people identify with their nation or country (e.g., I am an American or I am Irish or Chinese). This was not always the case. Prior to the emergence of a global system of nation-states, about 250 years ago, people primarily identified with their clan, tribe, village, region, or local religious sect. We now see the nation as a natural, coherent unit that should not be subservient to other political bodies. Yet, as East Asian historians Timothy Brook and Andre Schmid (2000, 12) noted, "The nation is only of consequence to the extent that it is apprehended as having immediate personal importance to those within it." Part of the nation's importance is that it gives people a sense of belonging and becomes part of their self-identity.

Many people feel an emotional bond with their nation or a national way of life. This feeling of patriotism implies a devotion and desire to improve the nation. It is easy to confuse patriotism with nationalism. Nationalism is the idea that the nation comes first. It can be a neutral term, describing the principle of organizing social-economic life around the nation or building up a nation. Or it can refer to a belief that one's own nation is superior to all others and in a competitive rivalry with them. Pride in nation can mean respect for one's national heritage. Alternatively, it can turn jingoistic, arrogant, and militaristic and imply looking down on people of other nations, races, or cultures.

Nationalism and national identity came to the forefront as East Asia moved beyond colonialism and foreign occupation in the twentieth century. Pride in nation has surfaced in many ways. It appeared as nations showcased their successes when hosting the Olympics, as in Japan in 1964, Korea in 1988, and China in 2008. People expressed pride in their country's achievements, traditions, language, history, and way of life. Pride in nation helped to fuel the East Asian economic miracle as people rallied around the nationalist ideal of creating an economically strong nation. As the political scientist Meredith Woo-Cumings (1999a, 23) remarked, "The cold war imparted urgency to the developmental projects in Northeast Asia, but in other ways it was not a *sine qua non* for the rise of the developmental state. What was critical was . . . the role of nationalism." Having achieved dramatic economic growth only enhanced further pride in nation. According to Yongnian Zheng, director of the East Asian Institute, National University of Singapore (1999, 2), "The revival of nationalism in China can be attributed to, among other things, its rapid domestic development. . . . A strong sense of national pride comes to average Chinese citizens, a sense probably as strong as, if not stronger, than what they felt when Mao Zedong declared the establishment of the Chinese Republic in 1949."

Nationalism's negative side often surfaces in periods of rapidly increasing uncertainty when people feel threatened. Pride in nation can turn into anger or arrogance. This appeared in East Asia as antiforeign protests, demonstrations, and legislation. At times "the West" has been the target; at other times, people directed nationalist anger toward East Asian neighbors.

Three issues have sparked East Asian nationalist fervor: fallout from Japan's actions during the Pacific War (1937–45), the economic rise of China, and continuing tensions with the United States.

The Japanese empire advanced across East Asia nearly seventy years ago, but its actions remain a source of tension in the twenty-first century. In surveys 96 percent of Chinese and 78 percent of South Koreans say Japan has not apologized enough for its wartime actions in Asia. A majority of Chinese describe Japanese people as violent, greedy, and dishonest. A visible sign of anti-Japanese feelings is seen in China's Museum of the War of Chinese People's Resistance against Japanese Aggression, established in 1987 and expanded in 1997 and 2005. China has seen several anti-Japanese demonstrations since 2005, with large countrywide protests erupting in 2010 after Japan seized a Chinese fishing boat captain in disputed waters.[14]

South Korea established the Seodaemun Prison History Hall museum to document Japanese atrocities during the colonial occupation. Although the past animosity between Japan and Korea may be fading, today's South Korean teenagers say that Japan is their country's primary enemy, and more pick Japan over China or North Korea as a threat.[15]

Tokyo's Yasukuni Shrine is a major national monument that honors Japan's war dead, including some who were classified as war criminals in the Pacific War. It includes a museum, the Yūshūkan, which depicts Japan as a liberator of Asia during the war. Several leading Japanese politicians have visited the shrine over the past decade, igniting serious diplomatic tensions with China and South Korea.[16]

Figure 6.5. Ultranationalist sound truck near the Yasukuni Shrine, Tokyo (Author photo).

Intraregional tension also has arisen over the "comfort women" issue. The term refers to as many as two hundred thousand young women and teenage girls who were forced to provide sexual services to the Japanese military during the Pacific War. Most were Korean, Chinese, or Japanese, but women from parts of Asia occupied by Japan during the war also were forced to into being sex slaves for Japan's military. As recently as 2007, Japan's prime minister and conservative politicians denied their existence.[17]

Japan's East Asian neighbors see visits to the Yasukuni Shrine by top politicians and the comfort women issue as evidence of the spread of extreme nationalism since the 1990s. There has been a surge of related activities, such as revising school history textbooks to downplay Japan's wartime atrocities and instill national pride, disciplining teachers who fail to show sufficient patriotism, requiring the frequent public singing of the national anthem and display of the national flag, and calls to remove Article 9—the "Peace" or antimilitarism clause—from Japan's Constitution. Ultranationalists drive regularly around Tokyo in loud sound trucks blaring extremist slogans and militaristic music. Over the past decade, as Japan's social and economic problems persisted while China's economic position soared, Japanese anxiety over China appears to have intensified.[18]

Beyond intraregional tensions, East Asia has a love-hate relationship with the West, especially the United States. At times East Asians admire the United States for its freedoms, energy, innovation, and wealth. At other times they see it as a global bully and fountain of moral decay. Large anti-American protests have taken place in Japan, Korea, and China. In 2005, 2009, and 2011, South Koreans mounted massive demonstrations (ranging from one hundred thousand to seven hundred thousand people) protesting trade agreements with the United States. In 2009, one hundred thousand Japanese protested U.S. military bases in Okinawa. Antiwestern protest movements have appeared in China. Despite these incidents, most

Japanese and South Koreans and many Chinese hold favorable attitudes toward the United States (see table 6.2).

South Koreans and the Chinese are not as positive toward Japan. The Japanese have a very low opinion of China; only 15 percent express favorable views (compared to 38 percent of South Koreans and 40 percent of Americans). The relationship between Taiwan and China is even more complex. Nearly one-half of Taiwanese believe the Chinese government is hostile toward the Taiwanese people.[19]

In East Asia, as elsewhere, national identity is neither static nor simple. People can identify with a nation by showing pride in national history, traditions, language, culture, and way of life, or by voicing opposition to perceived threats and enemies of the nation. A person can ground his or her identity by upholding national civic-legal institutions and ideals, or by acquiring a feeling of membership in a distinct racial-ethnic group. Mobilized nationalism can force leaders to bow to national ideals (e.g., justice, democracy), or it can justify wartime atrocities or the "ethnic cleansing" of minorities or neighbors.

Across East Asia national identity is multifaceted and constantly evolving. To be Chinese is be a part of a great ancient civilization, a population that is spread around the world, a huge modernizing multicultural society, the world's fastest-growing economy, and a rising

**Table 6.2. Percentage of Population with a Favorable
or Very Favorable View of the United States**

Country	2006	2012
China	47	42
Japan	63	72
South Korea	58	79
Canada	59	na
Germany	42	52
United Kingdom	55	60

Source: Pew Global Attitudes Project.

Note: na = not available.

Figure 6.6. Koreans protest a beef trade pact with the United States in 2008. Source: http://commons.wikimedia.org/wiki/File:080503_ ROK_Protest_Against_US_Beef_Agreement_05.jpg.

Figure 6.7. Japanese protest U.S. military bases in Okinawa in 2009. Source: http://commons.wikimedia.org/wiki/File:The_ protesting_crowd_in_Ginowan_on_2009-11-08.jpg.

international power.[20] To be Taiwanese is to be Chinese but distinct from the mainland Chinese.[21] Moreover, as China scholar and sociologist Thomas Gold (2003, 11) remarked, "[T]he conscious effort to define and articulate a distinct Taiwanese national identity has become a critical component of Taiwan's social, political, and cultural life. It is a signature aspect of the remaking of Taiwan in virtually all spheres of life since the end of martial law in July 1987." To be Korean is to belong to the Korean ethnic group with a long heritage, yet one that is overlaid with competing political divisions.[22] Debates about the meaning of being Japanese also have a long history, and it is changing. At various times it meant belonging to an ethnic-racial group, having a distinct cultural heritage, and supporting Japan's government in its relations with other nations.[23]

Ultranationalists in every country pursue one version of national identity. It is fear-based and centered on opposing globalization, foreign ideas or influence, and outsiders. Their influence with the national population depends on the flow of events, the degree of uncertainty about the future, and the power of informed, moderate voices. The meaning of being East Asian, or Chinese, Japanese, Korean, or Taiwanese, will continue to evolve in response to internal developments and relations with people in other parts of the world.

CONCLUSION

Sixty years ago few Americans had contact with or understood East Asia. Except for military personnel and a handful of tourists, few traveled there. Immigration from East Asia to the United States had all but stopped for half a century, and very few East Asian products reached U.S. shores. Today millions of people travel back and forth between East Asia and the United States each year. As of 2010 East Asia was the world region that sent the largest number of new immigrants to the United States. East Asian products flood U.S. stores, highways, and media outlets. Globalization has made the world a smaller place, and the distance between East Asia and United States has shrunk in innumerable ways. But, despite growing contacts and areas of convergence, differences will remain. The need to appreciate and understand those differences, as well as commonalities, is greater now than it has ever been.

NOTES

In addition to these notes, visit the AAS website at
www.asian-studies.org/publications/KIAS.htm
to view a full listing of works cited.

CHAPTER 1: EAST ASIAN HISTORY

[1] See Stanyon, Sazzini, and Luiselli 2009.

CHAPTER 2: EAST ASIAN CULTURE

[1] See Nisbett 2003.

[2] Some East Asians now celebrate western holidays, especially as commercial events (see Watson 1998).

[3] *Chuseok* is described in http://english.chosun.com/site/data/html_dir/2011/09/12/2011091200051.html (accessed on January 26, 2014).

[4] On Confucianism, see Littlejohn 2010; Rozman 1991; Tu 1996; and Yao 2000 (all listed in "Suggestions for Further Reading").

[5] The economic impact of Confucianism is discussed in Cha 2003; and Kwon 2007.

[6] On Daoism, see Littlejohn 2009 (listed in "Suggestions for Further Reading").

[7] On Buddhism, see Harvey 2012; and Smith and Novak 2004 (Novak listed in "Suggestions for Further Reading"). Also see Kane and Park 2009 on Christianity in South Korea.

[8] Ho (1976) discusses the concept of face.

[9] See Tsutsui 2010; and Economist 2010.

CHAPTER 3: FAMILY LIFE IN EAST ASIA

[1] On the Confucian family and its social practices, see Ebrey 1991, Ikels 1996, and Whyte 2004 for China, Park and Cho 1995 for South Korea, and Smith 1996 for Japan.

[2] See Peng 2012 on bloodline significance in China. Choe (1994) reported that 48 percent of South Koreans thought of bloodline when hearing the word *family* versus 9 percent of Americans; by contrast 53 percent of Americans think of love versus just 22 percent of South Koreans. Skinner (2002) noted that a man's child was legally and ritually considered as his main wife's child in the Chinese system regardless of birth mother. By contrast, in Korea, only the son of a primary wife could be a legitimate heir in the descent line. As Tsuya and Bumpass (2004a) noted, adopting males into a family that lacks a male heir has been long accepted in Japan. Janelli and Yim (2004) observed sonless Korean couples informally adopting sons-in-law, but this practice declined by the 1990s.

[3] Live-in "second wives" or concubines were common in nineteenth-century China, Korea, and Japan among wealthier families. For changes in dating and marriage practices, see Kendall 1996 on South Korea, White 2002 on Japan, Ikels 1996 on China, and Thornton, Chang, and Yang 1994 on Taiwan.

[4] Ruggles (2010) described stem versus joint families. Whyte (2004) discussed rural China's family structure. Unger (1993) reported that of urban Chinese families in 1982, 66 percent were nuclear, 24 percent stem, and about 3 percent joint (the rest were single-household or some other form), while in Taiwan the proportions were 56, 35, and 8 percent, respectively. He attributed the large proportion of nuclear families to migration, since migrants were unable to bring their extended families along. Weinstein et al. (1994) found 35 percent nuclear family, 32 percent stem family, and 26 percent joint family forms in Taiwan in the 1960s, but by the 1980s the respective proportions were 56 percent nuclear, 32 percent stem, and 7 percent joint. Sorensen and Kim (2004) found class variation in the family forms in Korea and no upper-class families. Half of all upper-middle-class families and 11 percent of working and lower-middle-class families followed the stem family pattern in the 1990s.

[5] *Filial piety* is written with the same character but pronounced *xiao, hyo*, or *kō* in Chinese, Korean, or Japanese, respectively. See Ikels 2004 for an overview and summary. As Hashimoto (2004, 182) argued, "Filial piety in East Asia today is at once a family practice, an ideology, and a system of regulating power relations." Also see Janelli and Yim 2004 and Wang 2004 on linkages between filial piety and "moral worth," rituals, and daily social practices in South Korea and China. Wang (2004) observed that into the twentieth century, China's government used filial piety as a justification for urging families to care for the elderly and minimize their reliance on state social services.

[6] On dating and mate selection, see Quah 2008, 14–20, for an overview. On Japan, see Hashimoto and Traphagan 2008; and Murray and Kimura 2003. Kumagi (2008, 34) noted that in 1933 roughly 69 percent of Japanese marriages were arranged and 13 percent were love marriages. By 1965 the two types were even, and as of 2000 about 87 percent were love matches versus 7 percent arranged. Hamabata (1990) noted the retention of arranged marriage practice among upper-class Japanese families, especially those that have extensive business interests.

[7] On declining arranged marriage in China, see Xia and Zhou 2003. Unger (1993) found that 30 to 50 percent of Chinese marriages were arranged prior to 1950, but less than 3 percent have been since the 1950s. Thornton, Chang, and Lin (1994) found a similar change in Taiwan and reported that in the 1950s, 62 percent of mate selection was by parents alone, 33 percent was a decision made jointly between the couple and parents, and 16 percent was by the couple alone. By the 1980s the respective percentages were 13 percent parents alone, 56 percent jointly, and 31 percent couple alone. Kim, Choi, and Park (1994) found dramatic changes in mate selection in South Korea. In 1959, 30 percent of adults said parents alone should decide on a daughter's husband and 60 percent said primarily parents, leaving about 10 percent saying it should be the daughter's decision. However, by 1990 only 3 percent said it was the parent's' decision alone and 18 percent said primarily parents, with most (80 percent) saying the daughter should decide. Sorensen and Kim (2004) report that most marriages in Korea today are love matches or half love and half arranged (see also Baldacchino 2008; and Kendall 1996, 94–110).

[8] According to Lee (2001) because secondary schools are single sex, South Korean universities function as "marriage markets."

[9] Most Japanese say they wish to marry (over 98 percent), but the singlehood rate is increasing (see Natsukari 1994). Raymo, Iwasawa, and Bumpass (2009) found Japanese cohabitation rates of 20 to 25 percent. This compared to rates of 3 to 8 percent just a decade ago. Raymo and Iwasawa (2008) noted that in Japan the proportion of first births due to premarital conceptions grew from 8 percent in 1975 to almost 30 percent in 2005, and nearly one in four first marriages in 2000–2005 was preceded by pregnancy. They attribute this to trends toward later marriage and earlier initiation of sex. Rindfuss, Choe, Bumpass, and Tsuya (2004, 855) noted, "Japan is in the midst of substantial family change. Delayed marriage is far advanced, and increases in nonmarriage may be underway." Also see Tsuya 1994 on changing attitudes about family in Japan. Cui, Li, and Gao (2001) and Ikels (1996) discussed changing attitudes regarding premarital sex in China. Thornton, Chang, and Lin (1994) reported that premarital sexual relations with a prospective spouse increased in Taiwan from 11 percent in the 1950s to 40 percent by the 1980s.

[10] Whyte (2004) reports much greater acceptance of remarriage after the death of a husband among Chinese than among Taiwanese.

[11] On family registration systems, see Krogness 2011; and Miyamoto, Shohey, and Kyon 2011. Chan and Buckingham (2008) and Cheng and Selden (1994) describe the *hukou* system.

[12] On Meiji Era changes in family law, see Cho and Yada 1994; Jansen 2000, 472; and Tanaka 2012. On the *ie* household, see Gotō 1994; Heine 1995; Moon 1998; and Sugimoto 2010, 156–88.

[13] See Nam 2010; and http://www.unhcr.org/refworld/topic,4565c22514,4565c25 f1df,47d6545fc,0,,,KOR.html. (accessed August 15, 2012).

[14] In the United States as of 2003, 63 percent of mothers with preschool-age children (younger than six years) were in the labor force. Of those mothers, 70 percent worked full time and 30 percent worked part time. http://mchb.hrsa. gov/mchirc/chusa_04/pages/0310wm.htm (accessed on January 26, 2014). In Japan, Taiwan, and South Korea, about 20 percent of women with young children (under six) work outside the home, but there are large differences. Tsuya and Choe (2004) found that in Japan 40 percent of mothers with pre-kindergarten-age children do not work outside the home, 29 percent work part time, and 31 percent work full time, while in Korea, 82 percent of mothers with young children do not work outside the home. Almost half (over 40 percent) of Japanese mothers with school-age children (over six years of age) do not work outside the home (29 percent work part time and 31 percent full time), while in South Korea, 83 percent of mothers with school-age children do not work outside the home. Brinton (2001a) noted that 39 percent of Japanese women worked part time versus 9 percent of Korean women and 6 percent of Taiwanese women. See Janelli and Yim 2004 on South Korean family size reductions, child care, and children's educational responsibilities.

[15] See Chen, Liu, and Mair 2011. Taiwanese families also rely on grandparents, relatives, neighbors, and babysitters (Yu 2001a). Pong and Chen (2010) found that children who reside with grandparents in Taiwan have positive academic performance outcomes, and Yu and Su (2006) learned that Taiwanese families have a preference for investing in the education of firstborn sons but not firstborn daughters.

[16] Kuroda (1994) contested the idea that most Japanese and Chinese families prior to the Second World War lived in three-generation households. He found that in 1920 just 29 percent of Japanese families and in 1930 48 percent of Chinese families were in three-generation households. Coresidence rates are not certain. Goodman (2002, 14) noted that 72 percent of Japanese over the age of sixty-four resided with at least one child in the early 1990s, but this declined to 60 percent in the 1990s. Bumpass (1994) found 1 to 2 percent of American and 10 to 30 percent of Japanese adults coresiding with a parent, yet Bumpass and Choe (2004) reported that in the 1990s nearly one-quarter of American adults in their fifties had a parent living with them. Kawabe and Shimizu (1994) reported 13 to 20 percent coresidence with elderly parents in the United States but 60 to 70 percent in Japan. Rindfuss, Choe, Bumpass, and Byuan (2004) reported rates of 28, 46, and 2 percent of married couples coresiding with parents in South Korea, Japan, and United States, respectively. In South Korea about 50 percent of persons over sixty years of age live with their sons and about 6 percent with their daughters. Bumpass and Choe (2004) reported that two-thirds of Korean but just one-third of Japanese eldest sons say it is the eldest son's duty to take care of aging parents. In China, Unger (1993) noted that most urban Chinese elderly (55 to 70 percent) do not wish to live with their children. Brinton (2001b) observed that three-generation households are twice as common in Taiwan as in South Korea or Japan. Coresidence with parents is not always due

to cultural factors. As Logan and Bian (1999) found in a study of urban China, preferences do not match behavior. About one-third of elderly Chinese said they are not living in their preferred or "best" situation. About one-half who were coresiding with children were doing so because of housing shortages or other factors, not preference. Of elderly Chinese living alone but wishing to live with their adult children, overcrowding was the main reason for not doing so. Kurosa (1994) found economic and practical factors to be significant in coresidence decisions in Japan. In China, Miller (2004) noted how elder care obligations usually fell to daughters. Sun and Liu (1994) reported high rates of Taiwanese newlyweds living with the husbands' parents (over 70 percent) into the 1980s with a slow decline over time. Compared to mainland China, Whyte (2004) found Taiwanese more likely to have live-in daughters-in-law, and those daughters-in-law were working full time or as part of a family business. Traphagan (2004) described how pressure for coresidence in rural Japan had reduced marriage interest by local Japanese women and indirectly contributed to men seeking foreign brides (also see Kumagi 2008, 43–47). Ikels (1993) reported that urban Chinese elderly persons "strategically" nurture filial piety to secure support from adult children.

[17] On networked families in China, see Davis and Harrell 1993; and Unger 1993. Rebick and Takenaka (2006) describe a similar pattern in Japan.

[18] Tsuya and Choe (2004, 77) reported, "Japanese and Korean parents are, in general, greater 'stake holders' in their children's life course than American parents."

[19] Brinton (2001a and 2001b) described the East Asian M curve. Fricke et al. (1994) found an increase in married Taiwanese women working outside the home from 8 percent in the 1950s to about 50 percent in the 1980s. Choe, Bumpass, and Tsuya (2004) reported that most married Korean women do not work outside the home (74 percent) versus 43 percent of Japanese and 34 percent of American women. In Japan and the United States, about 22 percent of married women work less than thirty-five hours per week, but just 3 percent of Korean women do so, leaving about 35, 44, and 22 percent, respectively, working over thirty-five hours per week. As Lee and Hirata (2001) noted, the dominant pattern in South Korea and Japan, which have highly gender segregated job tracks, is for women to quit full-time work on the birth of a child; this is much less the case in Taiwan. Yu (2005, 714) held that "A more family-friendly work environment not only allows Taiwanese women to remain in their jobs after marriage and childbearing, but may also encourage them to have more children . . . [thus the] greater incompatibility between work and family obligations that characterizes the Japanese employment system may explain recent trends in Japanese women's marital and reproductive behavior."

[20] Housework and women working outside the home vary widely. According to the Beneese Institute for Child Sciences and Parenting (2006), "Tokyo mothers show the lowest percentage in their demands for fathers' further participation

in both household chores and childcare: the household chores (Tokyo, 66.6%, Seoul 67.2%, Beijing 83.8%, Shanghai 74.8%, Taipei 93.4%); childcare (Tokyo 76.2%, Seoul 83.9%, Beijing 98.7%, Shanghai 97.4%, Taipei 97.0%)." Tsuya, Bumpass, and Choe (2000) and Tsuya and Bumpass (2004b) reported that Japanese husbands average 2.5 hours of housework per week versus 7.8 hours for American husbands. As Brinton notes (2001a), married women with education are more likely to work in Taiwan but not South Korea or Japan, and the full-time male-female wage gap is smaller in Taiwan than in South Korea or Japan. Brinton also observed that while over 55 percent of Taiwanese work in firms with fewer than thirty employees, the percentages in South Korea and Japan are 24 and 33, respectively. Whyte (2004) noted the much stronger presence of family-based businesses and related microinstitutions in Taiwan. Lee and Hirata (2001) and Yu (2001a, 2001b) attributed the flexible, family-friendly work relations for women in Taiwan to the country's many family-based, small firms. The long commutes and working hours are discussed in Brinton, Lee, and Parish 2001; Choe, Bumpass, and Tsuya 2004; Tsuya, Bumpass, and Choe 2000; and Yu 2001a. Workers average about seventy-five minutes of commuting time per day in Japan, thirty-two minutes in South Korea, and eighteen minutes in Taiwan, versus twenty-one in the United States. On Japanese egalitarian husbands, see Ishii-Kuntz 2003; and Nakatani 2006. Note that Tsuya and Bumpass (2004b) found little difference in housework contribution by egalitarian versus nonegalitarian Japanese husbands. Jolivet (1997) reported that 37 percent of Japanese fathers had no contact at all with their children during the workweek.

CHAPTER 4: SCHOOL AND THE TRANSITION TO WORK

[1] The international achievement tests are TIMSS (Trends in International Math and Science Study) and PISA (Program for International Student Assessment). See Lewin 2010; Institute of Education Sciences 2007, 2011; Lynn 1988; and Stevenson 1991.

[2] See Tobin, Hsueh, and Karasawa 2009, 67–68. Also see Lewis 1997; Peck 1991; Rohlen 1997; Stevenson and Lee 1990; and Tobin, Wu, and Davidson 1989.

[3] On Asian class sizes, see the following websites (accessed, except where noted, on January 26, 2014).

http://www.arthurhu.com/index/classize.htm

http://factsanddetails.com/china.php?itemid=1094&catid (accessed on January 15, 2012)

http://economix.blogs.nytimes.com/2009/09/11/class-size-around-the-world/

http://www.koreanbeacon.com/2009/05/18/why-is-the-south-korean-school-system-better/

http://www.oecd-ilibrary.org/education/education-at-a-glance-2010/what-is-the-student-teacher-ratio-and-how-big-are-classes_eag-2010-26-en

http://www.cato.org/pub_display.php?pub_id=5537

http://www.nier.go.jp/English/EducationInJapan/Education_in_Japan/Education_in_Japan_files/201109BE.pdf

Data from the OECD (Organization for Economic Cooperation and Development) show average primary school class sizes as being over 30 in 2000 in Korea and Japan. The NIER (National Institute for Educational Policy Research) report has Japan's primary enrollment data over time and shows average class size dropping to 25.2 in 2010. UNESCO (United Nations Educational, Scientific, and Cultural Organization) gives class size in 2007 as 30 for junior high school. See http://unesdoc.unesco.org/images/0021/002147/214735e.pdf (accessed January 15, 2012).

Class size and moral education are also discussed in Choi 2007; Cummings 1997; Kipnis 2011; Lanham 1986; Lewis 1995, 1997; Rohlen 1983; and Tobin, Hsueh, and Karasawa 2009, 35, 52.

[4] On teacher salaries and respect for teachers, see OECD, "Teachers' Salaries," Education: Key Tables from OECD, no. 6, 2011, and the following websites, all accessed on January 26, 2014.

http://economix.blogs.nytimes.com/2009/09/09/teacher-pay-around-the-world/

http://nces.ed.gov/pubs/eiip/eiipid40.asp http://nces.ed.gov/pubs2009/2009039_5.pdf

http://www2.ed.gov/about/inits/ed/internationaled/background.pdf

Chou and Ho (2007) suggest that Taiwan's teacher salaries are not high. See Ingersoll et al. 2007 on teacher preparation.

[5] High school and university entrance, and school-to-work transition is discussed in Brinton (2008), Choi (2007), Rohlen (1997), Seth (2002), Tsuneyoshi (2001) and Zeng (1999). On compulsory schooling, see http://chartsbin.com/view/xo6 (accessed January 26, 2014). Also see Lynn 1988; and Stern 1997.

[6] On entrance exams and the exam system, see Aspinall 2005; Okano and Tsuchiya 1999; and Zeng 1999.

[7] On the fact that students do not have higher suicide rates and may have equal or higher levels of satisfaction, see Lynn 1988; Stevenson and Lee 1990; Stevenson 1991; Tsuneyoshi 2001; and Zeng and Tendre 1998.

[8] On cram schools and supplemental education, see Bray 2007; Chen and Lu 2009; Chou and Yuan 2011; Dierkes 2011; Lee 2011; Okano and Tsuchiya 1999; Russell 1997; Seth 2002; Zeng 1999; and Zhang 2011.

[9] In 2007, the percentage of teens agreeing that money brings happiness in Washington, DC, was 45 percent, Tokyo 16 percent, Beijing 8 percent, and

Seoul 34 percent. See http://www.childresearch.net/RESOURCE/DATA/ SPECIAL/SIXCITIES/index.html (accessed January 26, 2014).

[10] On parental investments in schooling, see http://www.nationsencyclopedia. com/economies/Asia-and-the-Pacific/Japan-POVERTY-AND-WEALTH.html (accessed January 26, 2014). Also see Chan and Mok 2001; Mok 2006; and Slater 2010a).

[11] According to UNESCO, tuition and fees together average $3,200 per year at Japan's public high schools and $7,000 per year at private schools. http://unesdoc.unesco.org/images/0021/002147/214735e.pdf (accessed January 26, 2014).

[12] On gender divisions in Japanese higher education, see http://www.mext.go.jp/ english/statistics/ (accessed January 15, 2012).

[13] On Japanese educational reform, see Aspinall 2001; Eades, Goodman, and Hada 2005; Fujimura-Fanselow 1997; Goodman 2008; Mok 2006; Takayama 2007; and Tsuneyoshi 2001.

[14] On discouraged Japanese youths, see Brinton 2008; Eades, Goodman, and Hada 2005; Fujimura-Fanselow 1997; Genda 2005; Goodman 2011; Leheney 2006; Slater 2010a, b; Takayama 2007; and Tsuneyoshi 2001. Goodman (2011) discusses Japanese college students who attend vocational schools because they cannot find work. Kelly and White (2006) describe an emerging two-tier education system.

[15] On Korean schooling, see Choi 2007; Lee 1997; Lee 2000; Okano and Tsuchiya 1999, 28–31; Seth 2002; and Sorensen 1994. Also see *World Education News*, May 2002, "Recent Trends and Developments in Education in the Republic of Korea," http://www.wes.org/ewenr/02may/feature.htm (accessed January 26, 2014).

[16] On Taiwan, see Chen 1997; Chou and Ho 2007; Chou 2008; Jao and McKeever 2006; Lin 1983; Mok 2006; Wallace and Chou 2001; Wu 1997; and *The Statistical Yearbook of the Republic of China*, http://www.stats.gov.cn/ english/ and World Education News, May 2010, "Education in Taiwan," http://www.wes.org/ewenr/10may/feature.htm (both accessed January 26, 2014).

[17] China's schooling is discussed in Cleverley 1985; Hannum and Adams 2009; Hannum, Wang, and Adams 2010; Min 1997; Postiglione 2006; Turner and Acker 2002; and Wang 2003. Chan and Mok (2001) and Mok (2006) describe the rapid growth of private education in China. Also see http://gse.buffalo.edu/ org/inthigheredfinance/files/Country_Profiles/Asia/China.pdf (accessed January 26, 2014).

[18] See http://www.asianscientist.com/academia/chinas-higher-education- students-exceed-30-million (accessed January 26, 2014). *Christian Science Monitor*, "China Goes to College—in a Big Way," July 29, 2005; and http://gse.buffalo.edu/org/inthigheredfinance/files/Country_Profiles/Asia/China. pdf (accessed January 26, 2014).

[19] See Cummings 1997 on the J-Model.

CHAPTER 5: INEQUALITY AND DIVERSITY IN EAST ASIA

[1] See Chun 2011; and Kim 2012.

[2] See Choe 2005; Jones 2012; Kay 2011; Park 2004; and Yoon 2010. Two recent statutes are the Basic Law regarding the Better Treatment of Foreign Residents (2007) and the Multicultural Family Support Act (2008).

[3] See Brown 2004; Cooper 1996; and Ching 2001.

[4] See Alliance of Taiwan Aborigines 1995; Cauquelin 2004; Corcuff 2000, 2011; and Jao and McKeever 2006.

[5] See Bélanger 2010; Jones 2012; Lu 2011; Ngo and Wang 2011; Tang, Bélanger, and Wang 2011; Tsai 2011; and Wang and Bélanger 2008.

[6] On Japanese multiculturalism, particularly the Ainu and Okinawans, see Allen 2002; Befu 2001; Howell 1994, 2004; Lie 2001; Pearson 1996; Rabson 2012; Siddle 1996, 2009; Smits 1999; Walker 2001; and Weiner 2009.

[7] Bondy (2010) and Neary (2003, 2009) discuss the *burakumin* in detail.

[8] On Koreans in Japan, see Chung 2010; Iwabuchi 2000; Fukuoka 2000; Lie 2001, 2008; Min 1992; Ryang 1997, 2009; and Weiner and Chapman 2009.

[9] *Nikkeijin* are discussed in DeCarvalho 2003; Linger 2002; Roth 2002; and Tsuda 2003, 2009. Foreign workers are discussed in Douglass and Roberts (2000); Komai (2001); Mori (1997); and Shipper (2008). Foreign worker data are from the Statistics Bureau, Japanese Ministry of Internal Affairs and Communication.

[10] On foreign brides in Japan, see Bélanger 2010; Faier 2009; Jones 2012; Knight 1995; and Suzuki 2003. Also see Traphagan 2004 on northern Japan.

[11] For more on China's minorities, see Brown 1996; Csete 2001; Dikötter 1990, 1992, 1997; Harrell 1990, 1995, 2001; Hoodie 1998; Kaup 2000; Mackerras 1994, 2011; Mullaney 2011; Schein 2000; H. Wang 2002; and S. Wang 2003.

[12] On China's Muslim minorities, see Dillon 1999; Gillette 2000; Gladney 1991, 1994, 1998, 2004; and Lipman 1997.

[13] See Gustafsson and Shi 2003; Iredale and Guo 2003; Riley 2004; and Sicular et al. 2010.

[14] For a general discussion, see Barraclough and Faison 2009; Chang and England 2011; and Brinton 2001 a and b. On the impact of family obligations, see Zhang, Hannum, and Wang 2008.

[15] In addition to the sources listed in note 14, see Kagohashi 2006; Park 2007; and Yu 2009. Japanese women's part-time work is also discussed in chapter 3 of this booklet.

[16] On China's complex gender pay gap, see Chubb et al. 2008; Cohen and Wang 2009; Ha, Yi, and Zhang 2009; Li, Song, and Liu 2011; Magnani and Zhu 2011; Zhang, Hannum, and Wang 2008; and Zhou 2004. On gender job discrimination, see Gaetano 2004; Guang and Kong 2010; Li, Song, and Liu 2011; and Xin and Yihui 2011.

[17] See Cai and Lavey 2003; Gupta, Chung, and Shuzhuo 2009; Gupta 2010; and Riley 2004. On estimates and bachelor villages, see Penêda 2012; and Poston, Conde, and DeSalvo 2011.

[18] On changing levels of inequality in Japan, see Brinton 2008, 2010; Hara and Seiyama 2005; Hara 2007; Kosugi 2008; Ishida and Slater 2010; Sato 2007; Slater 2010b; and Yu 2012. Lett (1998) describes a different dynamic in South Korean inequality.

[19] See Gill 2001.

[20] On postreform changes in Chinese economic conditions and levels of inequality, see Davis and Wang 2009; Gao and Riskin 2009; Guthrie 1999; Lin 1997; Liu and Li 2006; Solinger 1999; and Whyte 2009, 2010b, especially 11–32. Bishop and Chiou (2004) compare inequality in China and Taiwan.

[21] As Lǚ stated (1997, 21), "The *danwei*, an enclosed, multifunctional, and self-sufficient entity, is the most basic collective unit in Chinese political and social order. . . . As a basic unit in the Communist political order, the *danwei* is a mechanism with which the state controls members of the cadre corps, monitors ordinary citizens, and carries out its polities."

[22] See Lǚ 1997; Lǚ and Perry 1997; Naughton 1997; and Zhou 2004.

[23] See Whyte 2010a; and Zhou 2004, especially 163–65.

[24] The 2002 estimate is from Frazier 2006. For comparison, in the United States in 2006, 16 percent of the work force was in the public sector, 8 percent in the nonprofit sector, and 75 percent in the private sector (Warren 2008). The 2006 estimate is from Szamosszegi and Kyle 2011.

[25] On change in rural China and rural-urban dynamics, see Oi 1999; Sicular et al. 2010; Unger 2002; and Walder 2002.

[26] See Wang 2010; and Whyte 2009, 2010a, 2010b.

[27] On changing stratification in China, including the place of the CCP, see Bian 2002, 2009; Davis and Wang 2009; Li and Walder 2001; Tsai 2007; Walder 2002, 2003; Walder and Hu 2009; Walder, Li, and Treiman 2000; Walder and Zhao 2006; and Zheng 1997. Whyte (2010b) and Wu and Treiman (2007) explore relations between the *hukou* and social-economic inequality. Dickson (2003) discusses "Red capitalists."

[28] For more on the floating population, see Riley 2004; Unger 2002; Wu 2010; and Zhang 2001. Chang (2008) and Gaetano (2004) provide a detailed account of female migrant workers.

[29] See Lee 2009; Han and Whyte 2009; and Whyte 2010a. Also see Bian 2009 on mobility. The percentage comparisons of China, Japan, and the United States come from Whyte 2010b, 83.

[30] Wang (2011) notes that East Asia once had economic growth with equality, but this has changed dramatically.

Chapter 6: Looking to the Future

[1] See Naughton 2007, 143, for more discussion.

[2] For an overview of reasons, see Campos and Root 1996; Haggard 2004; Preston 1998; Simone 2001; and Zhu 2009.

[3] Haggard (1990) examined the shift to an export-led growth strategy across East Asia. Also see Deyo 1987; So and Chiu 1995; Thompson 1998; Vogel 1991; World Bank 1993; and Zhang 2003.

[4] The rate was 360 yen = $1 between the Second World War and 1971. It rose to 280 yen = $1 in the 1980s, 100 yen = $1 in the 1990s. By 2012 you could get about 80 yen for 1 U.S. dollar. A key turning point was the 1985 international "Plaza Accord" (signed in the Plaza Hotel). The yen had been 242 = $1 before the accord and then quickly rose in value. Murphy (1997) discusses financial changes in Japan. For more on postwar Japan's economic development, see Kingston 2001; and Tabb 1995.

[5] In addition to Johnson 1982 on the developmental state model, see Henderson and Applebaum 1992; Fukui 1992; Wade 1990; and Woo-Cumings 1999b.

[6] For a short, simple description of the *keiretsu*, see Economist 2009. For a discussion of it as a form of business organization and its place in Japan's economy, see Gerlach 1992; Gilson and Roe 1993; and Lincoln and Gerlach 2007. Miwa and Ramseyer (2006) called the *keiretsu* a myth in a controversial book. Most scholars of Japanese business and economy questioned their argument as too narrow and inaccurate (see Alexander 2009; Ahmadjian 2008; Goddard 2007; Lincoln 2008; Morck 2007; and Murphy 2008).

[7] See Coates 2000; Evans 1995; Hall and Soskice 2001; Wade 1990; and Weiss 1998 on the issue of whether the developmental state is a distinct type of state-business relationship and type of advanced capitalism.

[8] Beeson 2004; Callon 1995; Cargill and Sakamoto 2008; Henderson 2011; Palley 2002; Tsukamoto 2012; Walter 2006; and Uriu 1996 discuss the shift away from a developmental state model in Japan and East Asia.

[9] For more on the *chaebol*, export-led growth, and business-government relations in South Korea, see Amsden 1989; Chang 2006; Clifford 1994; Economist 2003; Haggard, Lim, and Kim 2010; Janelli 1993; Koo and Kim 1992; Powers 2010; and Woo 1991. Haggard and Moon (1994) provide details on U.S. aid and state-business relations from 1953 to 1970.

[10] Taiwan's development state and economic growth are discussed in Gray 2011; Hsu 2009; Ma 2009; Tsai, 2001; Wang 1995; Welle-Strand, Chen, and Ball 2011; and Wu 2007. Also see Taipei Representative Office 2010 for information on Taiwan's recent investments in China.

[11] China's situation is discussed in Kojima 2006; Lin 2011; Naughton 2007; Palley 2006; Razmi 2008; Razmi and Blecker 2004; and Yao 2010.

[12] On globalization, see Albrow 1996; Held et al. 1999; Schaeffer 1997; and Waters 1995.

[13] On elderly suicide, see Chen et al. 2011; Liu 2009; Pritchard and Baldwin 2002; Shah 2010; and Shah, McKenzie, and Koen 2007. See Ikels 2004 on the relation between elder suicide and filial piety and Zhang 2010 on rural married women.

[14] Opinion data on South Korean and Chinese views on Japanese apologies and Chinese attitudes toward the Japanese are from the Pew Global Attitudes Project (www.pewglobal.org/question-search). On the museum, see http://www.beijing-visitor.com/index.php?cID=429&pID=2023; and http://www.1937china.com/enweb/20120621/8536.shtml. On anti-Japanese feelings in China, see "China Rejects Calls for Apology," April 17, 2005, BBC News, http://news.bbc.co.uk/2/hi/asia-pacific/4453055.stm; and "New Anti-Japanese Protests Erupt in China," April 16, 2005, Washington Post, http://www.washingtonpost.com/wp-dyn/articles/A58567-2005Apr16.html. On the 2010 protest, see "Thousands in Chinese Provinces Stage a-Japan Protests," October 18, 2010, Los Angeles Times, http://articles.latimes.com/2010/oct/18/world/la-fg-china-japan-protests-20101018; and "Anti-Japan Sentiment Gains Strength in China," September 22, 2010, Time, http://www.time.com/time/world/article/0,8599,2020721,00.html (all accessed January 26, 2014).

[15] According to Simpson (2011), "Asked about enemies, 44.5% chose Japan, 22.1% chose North Korea, 19.9% chose the United States, 12.8% chose China and 0.6% chose Russia, showing that 44.5% of teenagers believe that Japan is an enemy." On the museum, see http://www.visitkorea.or.kr/enu/SI/SI_EN_3_1_1_1.jsp?cid=268143 (accessed on January 26, 2014). Also see Sheen 2003 on Korean-Japan relations. On Korean nationalism, including Korean views of the United States and Japan, see Shin 2006.

[16] On the Yasukuni Shrine controversy, see Breen 2008; Deans 2007; and Takahashi 2007.

[17] On comfort women, see Min 2003; Tanaka 2002; Hayashi 2001; Hicks 1994; Ueno 1999; and Yoshimi 2000.

[18] For example, Shintaro Ishihara, governor of Tokyo since 1999, is noted for his antiforeign and ultranationalist statements. On the textbooks and rise of new Japanese nationalism, see Kingston 2008; Matthews 2003; Nozaki and Selden 2009; Schneider 2008; and Stronach 1995.

[19] The Pew Global Attitudes Project reports great Japanese distrust of China.

Also see "Japanese Public Opinion of China Slips to 7-Year Low: Survey," *Taiwan News*, June 20, 2012, http://www.taiwannews.com.tw/etn/news_content. php?id=1952011. Rigger (2003, n. 4) discusses Taiwanese fear of China (all accessed January 26, 2014).

[20] Chinese identity is discussed in Bajoria 2008; Dittmer and Kim 1993; and Zheng 1999.

[21] Brown (2004) and Wachman (1994) discuss Taiwanese national identity. Also see Gold 2003; and Rigger 2003.

[22] Kim (2005) and Shin (2006) discuss Korean identity.

[23] For a discussion of Japanese national identity, see Doak 1997; and Yoshino 1992.

GLOSSARY

Boxer Rebellion – 1898 Chinese rebellion against foreign influence, crushed by an alliance of Western armies (chapter 1).

Buddhism – Most widely practiced religion across Asia, which originated in Nepal around 500 BCE. It emphases detachment from the material world and showing compassion to all living things (chapter 2).

bushidō – Ancient Japanese warrior code of honor (chapter 1).

buxiban – Exam preparation or "cram school" in Taiwan (chapter 4).

chaebol – Large-scale corporations in South Korea operating in multiple industries that received strong support from the government (chapter 5)

Chinese Communist Party (CCP) – Political party founded in the 1920s, long led by Mao Zedong, which won the 1949 civil war and still rules mainland China (chapter 1).

comfort women – Women who were forced to provide the Japanese army with sexual services during the Second World War. Their existence has been denied by many Japanese leaders, leading to international tension and criticism (chapter 6).

Confucianism – A set of ethical principles and a way to organize government, community affairs, and social relations traced to Kong Qiu, who lived in China about 500 BCE (chapter 2).

Cultural Revolution – A decade of great social upheaval and anti-intellectualism in Mao's China (1966–76) (chapter 1).

danwei – Chinese term for the workplace and the institution of workplace services (chapter 5).

Daoism – A philosophy and set of religious beliefs originated in China that emphasizes harmony with nature (chapter 2).

daimyo - Japanese lord or ruler over lands (called *han*) in Japan's pre-Meiji era (chapter 1).

developmental state model – A model of government-economic relations first identified with postwar Japan, also called state-directed capitalism, in which the government actively guides the private sector to follow a plan of economic growth (chapter 6).

export-led growth policy – Policy to spur economic growth that emphasizes increased international trade, was associated with postwar Japan, and was seen as responsible for rapid East Asian growth in the 1970s–2000 era (chapter 6).

extraterritoriality – Treaty provision under which western foreigners in China (or other semicolonial areas) were exempted from local laws and punishments and only subject to the laws of their home countries (chapter 1).

fenjia – Chinese term meaning household division, referring to dividing property among several male heirs (chapter 2).

filial piety – Devotion and the moral duty of children to obey and care for parents based on Confucian values (chapter 3).

floating population – The millions of Chinese migrants who moved from rural areas to urban areas without legal permission under the *hukou* system (chapter 5).

furiita (also spelled *furitaa*, *freeter* or *freeta*) – Japanese term for young adults who stay in part-time jobs, implying that it is voluntary for the purpose of greater leisure time (chapter 5).

Great Leap Forward – Mao's disastrous attempt to speed industrialization in China; it produced a massive famine (1958–63) (chapter 1).

guanxi – Chinese term for personal connections (chapter 5).

hakwon - Exam preparation or "cram school" in South Korea (chapter 4).

han – Land areas in Japan's Tokugawa era ruled by a local lord or daimyo (chapter 1).

hangul – Korean writing system still in use, invented by King Sejong, based on an alphabet and sounds (chapter 1).

Hermit Kingdom – Nickname used by foreigners to describe Korea during the nineteenth century (chapter 1).

hoju – Korean head-of-family registration system introduced by the Japanese colonial government and abolished in 2005 (chapter 3).

hukuo – Chinese registration residence-permit system (chapter 3).

joint family – A household comprised of a main couple, possibly including their siblings and the spouses and children of their siblings; the adult children of the main couple; and their spouses and children (chapter 3).

J-Model – Japanese model of schooling linked to state-led economic development (chapter 4).

juku – Exam preparation or "cram school" in Japan (chapter 4).

ie – Traditional Japanese family based on the samurai family (chapter 3).

import-substitution policy – Policy meant to spur economic growth, often used by less-developed nations in the 1950s–60s, which focuses on domestic companies and limited international trade (chapter 6).

keiretsu – Families of the cooperating large companies and banks that dominate the Japanese economy (chapter 6).

keju – Ancient imperial Chinese civil service exam (chapter 4).

koseki – Japanese family registration system (chapter 3).

Kuomintang (KMT) – Chinese Nationalist Party, the leading political party from 1912 to 1949. It lost a civil war to the Chinese Communists in 1949 and then fled to Taiwan where it ruled until the 1980s (chapter 1).

kyoiku mama – Japanese term meaning "education mother" used to describe mothers deeply devoted to helping their children get an education (chapter 3).

lost generation – Description of young Japanese adults from the mid-1990s to the early 2000s (chapter 5).

Meiji era – Period of Japanese history (1868–1912) named after an emperor who modernized and industrialized the nation after its forced opening to West (chapter 1).

minzu – A nationality or ethnic group in China (chapter 5).

missing girls – A significant sex ratio imbalance in China, with more baby boys surviving due to male preference. Specifically it refers to girls who would be present if the sex ratio were balanced (chapter 5).

Nara era – The first major Japanese era (710–94), based in the city of Nara, in which central control began and Buddhism spread (chapter 1).

nikkeijin – Persons of Japanese ancestry from Latin America who returned to Japan (chapter 5).

Opium Wars – Wars between Britain and China (1839–42 and 1856–60) when China attempted to ban British imports of opium (chapter 1).

parasite single – Japanese phrase that is critical of young adults who do not marry or join the full-time work force (chapter 5).

patrilineal - Tracing family lineage or ancestry through the male line (chapter 3).

patrilocal – Practice in which a newly married couple resides with the husband's parents or moves to his village (chapter 3).

People's Republic of China (PRC) – China's official name after the Communist victory in 1949 (chapter 1).

primogeniture – Practice of ranking male children by age and giving most or all of the family inheritance to the eldest son (chapter 3).

qi – Also written *chi*, the essential energy or force in Daoist thought that influences eastern medicine and physical practices (chapter 2).

Red capitalist – Chinese Communist Party members who also own a private business (chapter 5).

Red Guards – Teens and young adults who joined in widespread destruction and terrorizing educated people in a mass hysteria of extreme devotion to Mao during China's Cultural Revolution (chapter 1).

rōnin – Japanese term meaning "lordless samurai." Today it refers to high school graduates who do poorly on a university entrance exam and delay entrance for one or more years while studying to retake it (chapter 4).

samurai – Members of Japan's warrior class during the pre-Meiji era (chapter 1).

shaman – a person who has special powers to see beyond the ordinary and reach altered consciousness and who is able to communicate with the spirit world (chapter 2).

shogun – Supreme military leader in Japan during the pre-Meiji era (chapter 1).

Shintō – Native Japanese religion that includes many spirits/gods called *kami* (chapter 2).

Silk Roads – Land and sea trade routes that connected China to Europe, India, and the Middle East for a thousand years (chapter 1).

spheres of influence – Name for large parts of China under American, British, French, German, Japanese, or Russian control in a scramble for wealth and resources in the nineteenth century (chapter 1).

stem family – Family form in which a couple and their eldest son plus that son's spouse and children co-reside in one household, common in East Asia into the twentieth century (chapter 3).

supplemental education – A system of private tutors and after-school "cram schools," mostly for junior high and high school students, which review school material, provide enrichment, or offer exam preparation (chapter 4).

Taiping Rebellion – Chinese rebellion (1850–64) against a weak, corrupt Qing dynasty that had allowed foreign influence in China, eventually crushed by the Qing forces (chapter 1).

Tokugawa era – A long period of Japanese history (1603–1868) characterized by isolation from the outside world but relative peace and prosperity. It ended with the Meiji era (chapter 1).

Yasukuni Shrine – Japanese war memorial that houses the remains of persons convicted of war crimes during the Second World War. Visits by Japanese politicians have led to international tensions with China and South Korea (chapter 6).

zainichi – Koreans living in Japan (chapter 5).

Suggestions for Further Reading

In addition to these Suggestions for Further Reading, visit the AAS
website at www.asian-studies.org/publications/KIAS.htm
to view a full listing of Works Cited.

Chapter 1: East Asian History

Bothwick, Mark. 2007. *Pacific Century: The Emergence of Modern Pacific Asia.*
Boulder, CO: Westview.

Ebrey, Patricia, Anne Walthall, and James Palais. 2009. *East Asia: A Cultural,
Social, and Political History.* Belmont, CA: Wadsworth.

Fairbank, John King, and Merle Goldman. 2006. *China: A New History.*
Cambridge, MA: Harvard University Press.

Frank, Andre Gunder. 1998. *ReOrient: Global Economy in the Asian Age.*
Berkeley, CA: University of California Press.

Jansen, Marius. 2000. *The Making of Modern Japan.* Cambridge, MA: Harvard
University Press.

Morton, W. Scott, and Charlton N. Lewis. 2004. *China: Its History and Culture.*
New York, NY: McGraw-Hill.

Murphey, Rhoads. 2009. *East Asia: A New History.* New York, NY: Longman.

Chapter 2: East Asian Culture

DuBois, Thomas D. 2011. *Religion and the Making of Modern East Asia.* New
York, NY: Cambridge University Press.

Littlejohn, Ronnie. 2009. *Daoism: An Introduction.* New York, NY: I. B. Tauris.

———. 2010. *Confucianism: An Introduction.* New York, NY: I. B. Tauris.

Liu, Xinru. 2010. *The Silk Road in World History*. New York, NY: Oxford University Press.

Rozman, Gilbert. 1991. *The East Asian Region: Confucian Heritage and Its Modern Adaptation*. Princeton, NJ: Princeton University Press.

Smith, Huston, and Philip Novak. 2004. *Buddhism: A Concise Introduction*. New York, NY: Harper.

Tu, Wei-Ming, ed. 1996. *Confucian Traditions in East Asian Modernity*. Cambridge, MA: Harvard University Press.

Yao, Xinzhong. 2000. *An Introduction to Confucianism*. New York, NY: Cambridge University Press.

CHAPTER 3: FAMILY LIFE IN EAST ASIA

Brinton, Mary C., ed. 2001. *Women's Working Lives in East Asia*. Stanford, CA: Stanford University Press.

Cho, Lee-Jay, and Moto Yada, eds. 1994. *Tradition and Change in the Asian Family*. Honolulu, HI: East-West Center.

Davis, Deborah, and Steven Harrell, eds. 1993. *Chinese Families in the Post-Mao Era*. Berkeley, CA: University of California Press.

East-West Center. 2002. *The Future of Population in Asia*. Honolulu, HI: East-West Center.

Goodman, Roger,, ed. 2002. *Family and Social Policy in Japan: Anthropological Approaches*. New York, NY: Cambridge University Press

Ikels, Charlotte, ed. 2004. *Filial Piety: Practice and Discourse in Contemporary East Asia*. Stanford, CA: Stanford University Press.

Perry, Elizabeth, and Mark Seldon, eds. 2010. *Chinese Society: Change, Conflict, and Resistance*. New York, NY: Routledge.

Quah, Stella A. 2008. *Families in Asia: Home and Kin*. New York, NY: Routledge.

Sugimoto, Yoshiro. 2010. *An Introduction to Japanese Society*. New York, NY: Cambridge University Press.

Tsuya, Noriko, and Larry Bumpass, eds. 2004. *Marriage, Work, and Family Life in Comparative Perspective: Japan, South Korea, and the United States*. Honolulu, HI: University of Hawai'i Press.

White, Merry Isaacs. 2002. *Perfectly Japanese: Making Families in an Era of Upheaval*. Berkeley, CA: University of California Press.

CHAPTER 4. SCHOOL AND THE TRANSITION TO WORK

Cummings, William K., and Philip G. Altbach, eds. 1997. *The Challenge of Eastern Asia Education: Implications for America.* Albany, NY: State University of New York Press.

Kipnis, Andrew B. 2011. *Governing Educational Desire.* Chicago, IL: University of Chicago Press.

Mok, Ka Ho. 2006. *Educational Reform and Education Policy in East Asia.* New York, NY: Routledge

Peterson, Glen, Ruth Hayhoe, and Youngling Lu, eds. 2001. *Education, Culture, and Identity in Twentieth-Century China.* Ann Arbor, MI: University of Michigan Press.

Postiglione, Gerard A., and Jason Tan, eds. 2007. *Going to School in East Asia.* Westport, CT: Greenwood Press.

Rohlen, Thomas, and Gerald LeTendre, eds. 1998. *Teaching and Learning in Japan.* New York, NY: Cambridge University Press.

Tobin, Joseph J., Yeh Hsueh, and Mayumi Karasawa. 2009. *Preschools in Three Cultures Revisited: China, Japan, and the United States.* Chicago, IL: University of Chicago Press.

Zeng, Kangmin. 1999. *Dragon Gate: Competitive Examinations and Their Consequences.* New York, NY: Cassell and Continuum Press.

CHAPTER 5: INEQUALITY AND DIVERSITY IN EAST ASIA

Brinton, Mary C. 2011. *Lost in Transition: Youth, Work, and Instability in Postindustrial Japan.* New York, NY: Cambridge University Press.

Chang, Leslie T. 2008. *Factory Girls: From Village to City in a Changing China.* New York, NY: Spiegel and Grau.

Davis, Deborah, and Feng Wang, eds. 2009. *Creating Wealth and Poverty in Postsocialist China.* Stanford, CA: Stanford University Press.

Gladney, Dru C. 2004. *Dislocating China: Muslims, Minorities, and Other Subaltern Subjects.* Chicago, IL: University of Chicago Press

Koo, Hagen. 2001. *Korean Workers: The Culture and Politics of Class Formation.* Ithaca, NY: Cornell University Press.

Weiner, Michael, ed. 2009. *Japan's Minorities: The Illusion of Homogeneity.* New York, NY: Routledge.

Whyte, Martin King, ed. 2010. *One Country, Two Societies: Rural-Urban Inequality in Contemporary China.* Cambridge, MA: Harvard University Press.

Yu, Wei-hsin. 2009. *Gendered Trajectories: Women, Work and Social Change in Japan and Taiwan.* Stanford, CA: Stanford University Press.

CHAPTER 6: LOOKING TO THE FUTURE

Cargill, Thomas F., and Takayuki Sakamoto. 2008. *Japan Since 1980.* New York, NY: Cambridge University Press.

Haggard, Stephan. 2004. "Institutions and Growth in East Asia." *Studies in Comparative International Development* 38 (4): 53–81.

Henderson, Jeffrey. 2011. *East Asian Transformation: On the Political Economy of Dynamism, Governance, and Crisis.* New York, NY: Routledge.

Naughton, Barry. 2007. *The Chinese Economy: Transitions and Growth.* Cambridge, MA: MIT Press.

Simone, Vera. 2001. *The Asian Pacific: Political and Economic Development in a Global Context.* 2nd ed. New York, NY: Longman.

Zhang, Yumei. 2003. *Pacific Asia: The Politics of Development.* New York, NY: Routledge.